<small>PRAISE FOR</small>
The Best Seat in the House

"This book inspired me and made me feel better . . . a lot better. Especially the part about the 'dark cloud lifting.' Allen Rucker tells us in a brilliant and funny way that there is no point in running from the truth, and if we go with it we are better off. Maybe even better than before."　　　　　—Teri Garr

"Lots of people can walk. Only Rucker could have written this book."　　　　　—Roy Blount Jr.

"A bitingly humorous, unobstructed view of life from the sitting position."　　　　　—Richard Cohen

"Allen Rucker has taken his own condition and expanded it to encompass the human condition. At once hilarious, heartwarming, thought-provoking, the man in the chair is on a roll."　　　　　—Martin Mull

"Uniquely honest, insightful, moving, and uplifting. This is an astoundingly good and important book."　　　　　—Ben Stein

"Honest, insightful, sometimes painful, but above all wryly funny . . . this is much more than a book about physical paralysis. Rucker has something to say to all of us about facing ourselves and getting on with it, and he says it straight."　　　　　—Harold Ramis

"Allen Rucker's *Best Seat in the House* is by turns very funny and deeply moving, both head-smart and heart-smart. Hats off."　　　　　—Richard Russo

"Rucker is a gifted observer-humorist, unleashing a straight-arrow honesty and a vibrant, penetrating wit while probing the most intimate aspects of contemporary life and human behavior."　　　　　—*Publishers Weekly*

"Very moving, not scary. [Rucker] is a talented man."
—David Chase, creator, *The Sopranos*

"Rucker has you laughing and crying at his exploits. . . . He is a smart man, and he used his intelligence to understand what was happening and to figure out problems. . . . Has you right in his head."
—*Philadelphia Inquirer*

"I loved Allen's book. . . . I hope you take the opportunity to read it. Allen's very genuine, emotional, and humorous insights . . . will hopefully provide you with some perspective and solace. . . . I greatly admire and respect Allen for his courageous work in writing this book."
—Sandy Siegel, president, Transverse Myelitis Association, *Journal of the TMA*

"His drollness peeks through and this book becomes a joy to read. . . . A man who learned to accept himself with humor, grace, and a keenly sharpened sense of the absurd."
—*Palo Alto Daily News*

"His writing talent is evident. . . . Offers compelling advice for people in a similar situation and thus is making a contribution to society despite his malady. More power to him!"
—*Daily Oklahoman*

"The book itself resonates with hope yet never stoops to preachiness or mush . . . genuine, fresh, sometimes startlingly direct. In the best possible sense of a horrible term, it truly is a feel-good book, the kind of book you don't just read but experience . . . passionate, moving, and flippant. I am rapt with admiration. And I'm not recommending the book as a favor to him, either; I recommend it as a favor to you."
—Tom Shales, *TVWeek*

"A savvy contribution. . . . Rucker is sanguine about being 'a front-runner in the race toward decrepitude and death.' . . . Ahead of the curve."
—*New York Times Book Review*, Editor's Choice

About the Author

ALLEN RUCKER is the author of seven books of nonfiction and humor, most of them written since he became paralyzed. He has written three books on the HBO series *The Sopranos*, including the *New York Times* #1 bestseller *"The Sopranos" Family Cookbook*. His other books include *The History of White People in America* (with Martin Mull) and *Redneck Woman* (with Gretchen Wilson). An award-winning TV writer, he lives in Los Angeles. For more information, visit www.allenrucker.com.

Also by Allen Rucker

Redneck Woman: Stories from My Life
(with Gretchen Wilson)

Entertaining with the Sopranos
(with Michele Scicolone)

Hollywood Causes Cancer: The Tom Green Story
(with Tom Green)

The Sopranos Family Cookbook
(with Michele Scicolone)

The Sopranos: A Family History

A Paler Shade of White
(with Martin Mull)

The History of White People in America
(with Martin Mull)

The Best Seat in the House

~

*How I Woke Up One Tuesday
and Was Paralyzed for Life*

Allen Rucker

HARPER

NEW YORK · LONDON · TORONTO · SYDNEY

HARPER

A hardcover edition of this book was published in 2007 by HarperCollins Publishers.

HarperCollins books may be purchased for educational, business, or sales promotional use. For information please write: Special Markets Department, HarperCollins Publishers, 10 East 53rd Street, New York, NY 10022.

FIRST HARPER PAPERBACK PUBLISHED 2008.

Designed by C. Linda Dingler

The Library of Congress has catalogued the hardcover edition as follows:

Rucker, Allen.
    The best seat in the house: how I woke up one Tuesday and was paralyzed for life / Allen Rucker.
        p.   com.
    ISBN: 978-0-06-082528-7
    ISBN-10: 0-06-082528-6
    1. Rucker, Allen—Health. 2. Paraplegics—United States—Biography. 3. Myelitis—Patients—United States—Biography. 4. Television writers—United States—Biography. I. Title

RC406.P3.R78 2007
362.196'8420092—dc22
[B]   2006041239
    ISBN: 978-0-06-082529-4 (pbk.)

08 09 10 11 12 ID/RRD   10 9 8 7 6 5 4 3 2 1

To Ann

The art of losing isn't hard to master;
so many things seem filled with the intent
to be lost that their loss is no disaster.

—"One Art," ELIZABETH BISHOP

CONTENTS

CONTENTS

INTRODUCTION

THIS IS A SLIM BOOK about paralysis. Actually, it's not really about paralysis. It's about a normal fifty-one-year-old man who becomes suddenly paralyzed for life. "Normal" may be stretching it, but before paralysis, my problems weren't a lot different from yours or your brother-in-law's. I wasn't raised by coyotes. I've never OD'd on drugs or embezzled money from WorldCom. I'm not a high-risk athlete, a daredevil, or a drunk. I didn't have this malady coming—it just came.

Paralysis itself, it turns out, is not that compelling a subject. What happens, at least in my case, is that you become paralyzed, half of you—from the waist down—doesn't work anymore, and life goes on. There are problems, for sure, but generally not life-or-death ones. I keep telling friends that paralysis in and of itself is no big deal, and they smile and shake their heads. They see this as a faint stab at humility. They think it's heroic to minimize something so profoundly life-altering and still keep on functioning. In fact, they rarely bring up their own problems in my presence. Or they bring them up, then quickly backpedal, saying things like, "I've got a lot of gall, talking about my shingles or my backache or my sex-change operation, to *you*. You're the one who's been given the really shitty deal. *You* should be the basket case."

These very friends, of course, were indispensable to me in getting through this "no big deal" of a crisis. And don't misunderstand—I'm not trying to equate paralysis with a canker sore. It's a terrible twist of fate, and I wouldn't wish it on an enemy, but there are degrees of difficulty in illness as well as in Olympic diving. I am not, say, the late Christopher Reeve. People tell me all the time that they couldn't handle my situation. I doubt that they would even dare to contemplate his situation. Right after I became paralyzed, I mentioned my admiration for Christopher Reeve to a correct-thinking liberal friend, and her response was, "I'm so sick of hearing about *him*, always promoting his own cause. What makes his illness any worse than anybody else's?" I was dumbstruck. I guess she thought he was playing the paralyzed-from-the-neck-down card for all it was worth.

Unlike the severely ill or impaired, I have a benign life-altering condition. First off, I have no chronic pain—that's a major blessing right there. No embarrassing spasms. No slurring of words, no disconnection between hand and brain, no emaciation. And unlike many of those with ALS, MS, cystic fibrosis, late-stage diabetes, cancer, or a host of other diseases, no inevitable degeneration and/or progression toward death. I am not in the throes of something that will finally reduce me to a shrieking invalid, flailing about in pain and confusion, wondering aloud, "Hey, whose life is it, anyway?"

I am paralyzed, a T-10 paraplegic. I spend my life in a

wheelchair and have done so for nine years. Such a sudden change of life can definitely shake you up. This book is about how I specifically got shook up.

Here's how it happened: I was lying around one Tuesday afternoon, avoiding work and nursing what I thought was a sore throat, and something hit me like a flaming meteor out of the sky. All so-called creative people, if not all people, period, wait in earnest for a bolt of lightning to strike them, to tell them what to do next. "Move to California!" "Divorce that woman!" "Buy a Buick!" My bolt of lightning came in the form of a sudden excruciating pain. It was an intense burning sensation around my waist, a ring of subcutaneous fire, which lasted for about three minutes. It was followed by a strange state of physical discomfort, between full-body sensation and half-body paralysis, that lasted for an hour and a half. That was it. Ninety minutes later, I had no feeling, no movement, no nothing from stomach to toes. Dazed and paralyzed.

It was a genuine catastrophe, preceded, given my particular mental makeup, by years of anticipating a genuine catastrophe. I, like millions of Americans, was an inveterate catastrophizer. I was forever in a state of suspended anxiety, girding for something terrible to happen and ruin what little sanity or stability I had acquired. "Hello, Mr. Rucker, your son has just been arrested as a terrorist," or "Hello, Mr. Rucker, you must repeat high school." In other words, I kind of knew something like this was coming. I just didn't know that *this* was coming.

What happened, in my case—I can't speak for anyone else with paralysis or any kind of disability—was that I became paralyzed and then had no choice but to get on with my life in ways that had eluded me before. It was kind of a malicious litmus test. Are you this or are you that? It was a fill-in-the-blank sign from somewhere, a reshuffling of the deck, a new "journey" in the Joseph Campbell mode, an excuse to start over. Of course it was also an excuse to give up and check out—in fact, the best excuse I've ever come across to lounge around in your underwear, stop bathing, and whine about the unfairness of it all. You become permanently paralyzed, and heroin becomes a viable, and attractive, option.

"Hey, what happened to *him*?" "Oh, you know, he woke up one day and was paralyzed for life." "Jeez ..." "Yeah, now he never leaves the house, spends all day watching ESPN, smokes a lot of dope, and talks about writing a book about becoming paralyzed that he'll never finish. Friends give him money, because, you know, the whole situation is awful." "I'd shoot myself." "Tell me about it. I'm on my way to church right now."

Two years into this thing, I developed some nasty sores on my feet and legs, the result of not paying attention to the half of my body that has no feeling. In the world of the sick, we call these bedsores, ulcers, or problem wounds. They were deep, they wouldn't heal, and they constituted a playground for bacterial infection. After I'd made a couple of trips to the hospital with a 104-degree temperature—caused by the inevitable infection—a smart nurse turned me on to a tissue-healing process called hyperbaric oxygen therapy (HOT). I went to see an expert in the field, Dr. Ralph Potkin, and he put me on an aggressive HOT program at his Beverly Hills facility. This involved lying in a completely sealed-off glass coffin of pressurized oxygen for an hour and a half every day, watching *Law & Order* reruns, and feeling sorry for myself. The therapy worked, at least on the wounds. Eighty sessions later, they had healed up nicely.

Along the way, hanging out daily at Dr. Potkin's treatment center, I bumped into the noted sixties spiritualist Baba Ram Dass (previously Richard Alpert), author of the classic new-age treatise *Be Here Now*. He was now just Ram Dass, or RD, and he was doing daily hyperbaric therapy to manage the aftereffects of a stroke that had felled him a couple of years before. He had trouble walking and talking, but he was always smiling; his smile was powerful. He was there at four o'clock. I was there at four o'clock. We struck up a tentative acquaintance.

Soon bumping into Ram Dass became the most important part of my day. I sensed that behind that beatific smile he knew something I didn't know, something that might help me transcend this awful plague that had struck me down. I was looking for a little karmic encouragement, a positive bolt of inspiration after such a negative one. I was angling for some *darshan*, as the Hindus call it—transformation by being in the presence of a holy one. So every day I would hop into the hyperbaric tank and wait for RD to arrive. Maybe we would talk. Maybe he would become my friend and direct me on a different path.

We never became friends, just passing small-talkers, but the last time I saw him, we had a long chat about our respective conditions. He asked me how I was doing and I said that I had no idea. Two years after the "incident," I was still in a stupor. The only tool in my emotional arsenal was denial. Lie low and don't think about it. Maybe the thing will resolve itself.

Ram Dass said he had felt the same kind of dejection and confusion for a while, but then, after some thought, he had found his new condition "interesting." Not tragic, not unfair, not unbearable, not the hardest thing he'd ever had to deal with, but "interesting." "I see it as a new incarnation," he said. "I'm looking forward to what might happen."

"New incarnation" sounded good to me. I wasn't all that happy with my old one, frankly, and I began to see how I could now revisit bigger questions than walking—my relation to myself, my wife, my family, my work, the mysteries of the universe—from a totally new perspective: four feet five inches tall, sitting in a wheelchair. Actually, I didn't need to make a long checklist; dealing with those things in a new way was pretty much required. "You have to do something, man—you're paralyzed!"

What follows is an account of my own Babaesque change, phase by phase, humiliation by revelation. This inevitably invites some thorny issues like aging, despair, wheelchair ballroom dancing, and sex. Everything, as they say, is now on the table. As I turn around and see this great horde of baby boomers behind me, 76 million strong, slouching toward AARP status, I think that maybe I'm just a little ahead of the game in the life-altering-illness/change-your-ways sweepstakes. Very, very few people in this demographic will get exactly what I have; it's a neurological disorder that strikes something like one to four out of every 1 million Americans. As I am fond of telling my friends, just by knowing me, you won't get *this*, but you'll probably get something—a heart attack, cancer, diabetes, MS, Alzheimer's, phlebitis, something— and it will spin you around in ways you cannot predict or prepare for.

Or maybe you'll be one of the lucky few and avoid The Big C and all those other abrupt life-benders and just get, you know, old. And you will get old, I promise. Inevitably, you'll start to walk funny, ask people to repeat things three times, pull your pants up too high, doze off during *Jeopardy!*, and probably have some chronic mechanical breakdown, like weak bladder control or painful arthritis. I know there are many fanatically health-conscious boomers out there thinking, Sure, that fat ass over there eating that double Whopper is going to keel over any minute, but I am going to maintain this wheat germ and 10K regimen and never get old. Well, I trained for 10Ks up to a few weeks before I became paralyzed and planned to run a hundred more. I loved to work out. I saw myself as the last person in the world to get sick. I had never been seriously ill or impaired. The last time I had occupied a hospital bed was in 1959.

I'm not that old myself, thank you, but by becoming paralyzed at fifty-one I've gotten an early peek at what's coming. In fact, the people out in the world who relate to me best are the old and lame. In a crowded, handicapped-unfriendly supermarket, for instance, Gramps and I will get shuffled to the side while our companions do the shopping. "So, young man, where'd you get that nice wheelchair?" he'll ask me. "Medicare buy it for you?" When I tell him that I'm not eligible for Medicare, for *years,* he'll smile a knowing smile, as if to say, "You will be soon, smart boy, you will be soon. "

The other people who most often query me about my condition are much younger, much healthier, and seemingly unconcerned about issues of decrepitude. Old age is not their worry, except for perhaps the aging of their parents, but they've lived long enough to know that life throws you curveballs and knuckleballs and an occasional high inside fastball that bonks you in the head. (Baseball pitches can be used to describe anything badly.) These people are trying to figure out how they would deal with something like this if, God forbid, it happened to them. I am a specter of their own demise. I invariably tell them that if they get hit like me, they'll probably do fine. They rarely believe me.

Frankly, I wouldn't have believed me, either, until this happened to me. It's both hard to contemplate something you've never experienced and hard to experience something you've never contemplated. Lots of people around you will be happy to tell you how to raise your kids or do better on the job or straighten out that golf swing. Few people, support groups aside, will advise you on how to be sick or impaired. Most don't know; others know that it is an experience unique to the participant and that you do best when you figure it out in your own way, in your own time.

Save a miracle of science, I will never walk again. I will never again do anything under my own control that involves any part of my body from the T-10 vertebra (or midsection) on down. Half of my body—feet, toes, legs, sex organs, etc.— is just along for the ride from now until death. But, despite this incontrovertible fact, it turns out, nine years and counting, that this crippling paralysis, this awful thing that makes others cringe or cry or fear for their own susceptibility, has in fact been a watershed event that has brought me, strangely, more peace of mind than I can ever remember. I won't make your skin crawl by saying it's a "blessing in disguise." It's not a blessing and there is no disguise. But there are things to be gained and things to be lost, and on certain days, I'm not sure that the gains are not as great as, or even greater than, the inevitable losses.

*　　*　　*

One last note: a lot of titles for the book were rejected on the way to *The Best Seat in the House*, which, of course, is any seat if you are alive and carrying on. Some were discarded with regret—*A Farewell to Legs*, for instance, or *Spinal Destination*. One candidate—*Between FDR and Perfect*—came from my neurologist, the droll Dr. Daniel Rovner. About a week after I was diagnosed with the rare and mysterious paralytic disorder transverse myelitis, and was completely freaked out, I asked him with tears in my eyes, "Seriously, Dr. Rovner, tell me the truth—what is really going to happen to me?" He thought for a moment, then answered.

"I can promise you this," he said, "you'll end up somewhere between FDR and perfect."

And he was about right.

The Best Seat in the House

ONE

SUDDEN ONSET

PLEASE DON'T GET ME WRONG. Living with paralysis is not like the disease-of-the-week TV-movie in which the Robert Urich character, having wrestled his demons to the ground for two commercial-filled hours, bravely gets off the floor and Frankenstein-walks across the room while his wife weeps and prays in the corner. I wish it had worked out that way, but it didn't. Paralysis is an often painful and confusing process that takes way more than two hours to get a handle on, and unlike a TV potboiler, the outcome is always in doubt. Just when you think it's time to bring up the music and roll the credits after a small victory—boom!— something untoward happens and you're reeling again. Sometimes you're lost, sometimes you're not, but you're never quite out of the woods.

Here is my life the day I became paralyzed. I was fifty-one, married with two sons, one in college and an eight-year-old at home, living in a big house in West Los Angeles, and pursuing my so-called craft as a writer of television specials and documentaries. I was at best an aging young Turk and at worst an aging journeyman, i.e., hack. I had made whatever mark I had made doing fringe television. First, in the 1970s, I was part of a guerrilla video group called TVTV (aka Top Value Television) which made satirical documentaries about public events like the Republican National Convention, the Super Bowl, and the weird seventies cult following of a fifteen-year-old Indian pop mystic named Guru Maharaj Ji. These shows were smart and well constructed and received a fair amount of critical acclaim. They didn't make any money, unfortunately, and the group broke up in 1977.

My next fringe success was a series of cable shows starring Martin Mull called *The History of White People in America*. Done on a shoestring, like TVTV, and featuring an all-star comedy lineup—Fred Willard, Mary Kay Place, Harry Shearer, and Michael McKean, with Martin as the David Attenborough of whiteness—this quirky faux-documentary look at mayonnaise-eating midwestern WASPs won awards and spawned two books, a line of greeting cards, and a tribute from the Museum of Television and Radio. I thought *White People* was my ticket out of the showbiz ghetto, but I was mistaken. Before it had reached the commercial radar screen, it faded. It became a small-c "cult classic."

But I did get my shot at the big Hollywood Lotto. With film director Amy Heckerling, I produced a television spin-off of *Fast Times at Ridgemont High* that lasted seven shows. I got my shot at writing and producing my own sitcom for

HBO about working-class misfits starring Dwight Yoakam. (The pilot didn't quite work.) I got my shot at writing an original HBO movie called *Hometown Boy Makes Good*, a story of a guy who fakes medical school to please his small-town parents. (Anthony Edwards was great as the lead, but the movie disappeared without a trace.) I wrote other pilots and other movies, and they all went nowhere. By the early 1990s I had no career. I was just another schmuck in Hollywood, looking for any low-end assignment to pay the rent.

"Write a tribute show about a campy old TV series I've never seen and couldn't care less about? Sure, I'll do that. Sounds like fun!"

Actually, writing one-shot shows I didn't much care about gave me a new professional life. I started to bounce back as a "specials" guy. I wrote now-you-see-them-now-you-don't network specials, even some about campy old television series, like *Brady Mania: A Very Brady Special*. I wrote a music special about the 1970s and a nostalgic look back at *All My Children*. During the heyday of hard-hitting trash-reality fare, I helped write *The World's Worst Drivers, Part Two* (I had nothing to do with *Part One*). It wasn't the stuff of Peabody Awards, but I occupied a marginal niche in the Dream Factory.

This eventually led to awards show writing, a strange form of literary harlotry—part comedy, part exposition, part shameless cant. The acclaimed television producer Don Mischer aptly described this job as the TV version of skywriting. People see it for a split second, then go back to sunning on the beach. It's the kind of writing where if you do it well, no one notices. If you do it poorly, then the third-tier TV actor reading your words for the first time off the TelePrompTer at the awards show will look out at 10 million people and say, "Hey, who wrote this crap?"

At first it was fun making up silly comedy bits for free-wheeling shows like the *CableAce Awards*, but a career of composing interstitial patter for splashy Hollywood ego fests is a career only a masochist could love. Struggling to come up with something clever beyond "Hubba-hubba, that is some dress!" or "Isn't this exciting? I can't wait to open this envelope!" for wit-challenged movie stars and then having their publicists give you comedy notes is like grabbing the short straw in the prison gang-bang sweepstakes. "You know, Phyllis doesn't think this copy is very funny and really wants to say something funny, so could you come up with something, you know, funny for her to say? Oh, and mention her new pantyhose commercial. Say something funny about *that*."

My greatest humiliation in this field came the night of my first assignment writing the annual special the *People's Choice Awards*. First off, this is a crowd-pleasing show, but it's not the Oscars. As an incentive to get stars to show up and thank "all you wonderful people out there, real, God-fearing people, the only critics who really count," the producers tell the winners in advance that they've already won. On this particular night, *ER* was a big winner and Anthony Edwards was a presenter as well as a recipient. I had written something for him to say. I don't really remember what it was, but (1) it wasn't very much and (2) it wasn't very funny (I'd already expended my store of zippy patter on the cast of *Friends*). Having known Anthony Edwards from the movie I had written seven years earlier, I started to approach him in the audience before the show. Just as I was about to tap his shoulder, I heard him tell a cast mate, loudly, as he held up my script page, "God, why do they give me this shit to say? I am not saying it." If I had had a gun, I would have stuck it in my mouth at that moment and pulled the trigger. He then turned, saw me, said hello, and upon discovering that I had written that particular line of shit, he smiled, said it was fine, and backed away as if I were a leper. I'm sure he walked off shaking his head, saying to himself, "Man, how sad is that? To be reduced to *this* ..."

The payoff for this period of marginal hackdom was a short-lived morning talk show with George Hamilton, a man known largely for his tan, and Alana Stewart, a woman known largely for her association with celebrated men like George. George and Alana, for those who don't read *People*, were once married, then divorced. Then Alana married the rock star Rod Stewart, then they got divorced. *George and Alana*, the show, was the world's greatest two-line pitch—"They're divorced, see, so they go on TV every morning and fight and bicker just like divorced people! It'll be a hoot!"

It was not a hoot.

It started out fine. George Hamilton is a genuinely funny guy who trades on being himself and making fun of himself at the same time. He is a Zen master of the superficial details of life that most of us never get around to caring about, like how to get a tan on a cloudy day, how to organize your clothes for maximum efficiency (George uses one of those electric conveyer belts you see at the cleaners), or how to keep the crease in your pants on the long drive from home to the red carpet. The answer to this last braintwister: don't put the pants on until you walk out the door; then keep your legs straight during the limo ride—excellent advice. George and I hit it off when I suggested that the first show begin with George, in a tux, standing out on Sunset Boulevard and holding a big sign reading "Maps to My House."

Unbeknownst to most people, including many actors and performers who sign up to do them, talk shows are hard work. You have to write and perform comedy bits, come up with zippy features like giveaway contests, and plot out topics of conversation. Most important, you have to actually know something about your guest and what he or she is there to talk about. There is homework to do, books to read in a night, movies and plays to see. Reading the *New York Times* on a daily basis also helps. Alana had very little actual show business experience; and George was, at heart, a late-studio-period movie star not used to working fourteen- to sixteen-hour days, the typical workday of a daily talk show host. Alana held up pretty well. George seemed to get bored quickly.

As Alana pointed out repeatedly, George just wanted to talk about George—that was his idea of a "talk" show. Alana just wanted to talk about her teenage kids and her out-of-control dog and her Chinese doctor appointments—you know, just like Kathie Lee or Kelly—but it didn't come out quite right. It wasn't cute or homey. There was no adorable kid around like Kathie Lee's son Cody to make the nation-wide audience—primarily of housewives—tear up with maternal pride. Alana was a shrewd, hardscrabble, model-thin beautiful Texas gal, not a maker of cookies. And anytime George tried to say or do something funny, Alana would sabotage it and think *that* was funny. The two of them, truth be told, were interested only in the guests who were certified heavy hitters, like Elton John or Farrah Fawcett. Unfortunately, not enough of those A-listers showed up to make the show interesting either to the divorcees or the American public.

It got so bad that Alana even refused to sample the food made by guest chefs during the cooking segments because her diet didn't allow for items like jambalaya or pizza Margarita. Once George ran out of stories about playing Dracula or the time he sunbathed out a hotel window in Rome, the show had nowhere to go. George had a great office, though—art deco furniture, a walk-in wine closet, and a humidor. It was like a suite at the Plaza.

For reasons that were never quite clear, executive producers for *George and Alana* came and went, beginning with the creator of the show and its biggest fan, Paul Block. As the ratings sank into oblivion, the guest list fell to the level of second-rate advice givers and Alana's dangerously unruly dog. The last straw was George challenging Howard Stern to a fistfight for describing him on the air as a vapid Hollywood no-talent (which he isn't). Howard didn't bother to respond.

Rick Moranis used to do a devastating parody of the talk show maven Merv Griffin on the classic sketch-comedy series *SCTV*. Rick's Merv, with his obsequious manner and his huge heinie sticking out of his sports coat, would match up guests like Yasir Arafat and Loni Anderson and then ooh and aah over the lining of their jackets. That is what *George and Alana* felt like five days a week.

By the third producer in thirteen weeks—a man who went out of his way to humiliate the show's announcer/sidekick, Gary Kroeger, and me, but didn't fire us because he thought it might upset the stars (who couldn't have cared less)—I had lost all sense of self-respect and professional worth. I was there every day, taking senseless abuse from a staff of low-end Hollywood mercenaries, and doing it for—just like them—the money! My only salvation was the knowledge that the show would soon suffer a merciful death and the residuals would keep me going for a while. My brain waves flatlined during this show. I was in a creative vegetative state.

Along with many deluded also-rans in Hollywood, I kept thinking I had a showbiz career, albeit a lowly one, but even that was largely a fiction. TV specials, not to mention fatuous talk shows, come and go, and people who write them are equally dispensable. Some writers find a groove crafting material for particular stars and milk it for years. They are the ones whose skills match the job and you can count their number on one hand. The rest of us are often like the shows we write for—one-shots. For whatever reason—age, talent, attitude, whatever—I was easily forgotten in the let's-try-someone-new mentality of network brainiacs.

But I was still hanging in there, with no idea of what else to do, and 1996 was actually a good year. I wrote more awards shows, including a fly-by-night, pay-you-in-the-parking-lot scam in Las Vegas called *The World Travel Awards*; got to work on some great live shows at the 1996 Olympics in Atlanta; and I collected residuals from *George and Alana*. We even took a family trip to Sweden, our first vacation in eight or nine years. There was always the inevitable panic between jobs, but that went with the territory. We were doing fine.

Then one day—December 10, 1996—I became paralyzed. Like the day Elvis died or OJ was acquitted, it's not something that you forget. It gets stuck in there for good.

On that fateful Tuesday, I was mostly thinking about an arthroscopic procedure on my right knee that was going to happen two days hence. This small, in-office operation was important to me. It would fix some torn cartilage in my knee so that I could soon start running again after a two-month hiatus. I loved to run. I had been running almost continually since college.

I was on the bed, reading an old issue of the *New Yorker*, and nodding out, when my legs suddenly started aching and tingling at the same time. The sensation began in the back of the thighs and moved to the waist. Then a sharp pain hit my midsection. It was excruciating but also diffuse, inexact, and short-lived. Imagine being branded by an around-the-waist branding iron.

After that sharp pain came and went, my first reaction was a general uneasiness, which forced me to move around to outmaneuver the now intermittent numbness and tingling. I got up from the bed and walked around the room, not weak or wobbly but just bothered to distraction by a discomfort that I couldn't describe, even to myself. I tried to relieve my physical uneasiness by sitting on the couch and putting my legs over the armrests. That didn't work. Then, thinking I had strained a back muscle or experienced a weird back spasm, I lay on the floor. That didn't do anything, either. I was no longer in any pain, but I was in an odd state of restlessness and apprehension. I knew this was virgin physiological territory but didn't announce it. Nobody likes a whiner who can't describe what the hell he's whining about.

My wife, Ann-Marie, came in after a hard day of teaching and offered an instant, ready-made diagnosis, partially predicated, I'm sure, on the fact that I was lying in bed on a weekday afternoon, didn't have a job, and didn't seem particularly sick. The aches and pains associated with flu, she said. It sounded right. I'd thought of this myself, later to realize that this was part of a mutual-denial game she and I had perfected after some very rough years: "Nothing's wrong. Everything's fine. Not to worry." I headed for a warm bath, anxious to soak my way through my condition.

The bath just increased the irritating tingling, and I had an overwhelming urge to keep moving. Later I thought: Was this the healthy nerves in my back telling the damaged nerves in my legs, "Hey, you have only a few minutes to keep functioning, you idiots, so don't sit around a bathtub. Walk! Move! Tap-dance!" I kept getting weaker. Out of the bath, I wobbled a bit and headed back to bed. Call your doctor, Ann-Marie said, if that will make you feel better. I did, and he wasn't in, but one of his associates gave the same diagnosis as Ann-Marie: a nasty flu virus of some kind. Take two aspirin and a warm bath. I didn't tell him I had already tried the bath treatment. I was sure that I was overreacting and that if I said anything hysterical, I would sound like a fool. Also, being from the American Midwest, I hated to be sick. In general, when people get sick, so my Calvinist forebears taught me, it's a sign of weakness or laziness, or a cry for attention. When people *make* themselves sick—which I thought was exactly what I was doing with all my consternation—they are gutless bellyachers of the first order and should be made to work overtime.

So Ann-Marie left to go to the dentist, I took two aspirin and got back into bed. The progression then began a fierce descent. One more trip to the same bath, a good fifteen seconds of immersion, and out in a flash, weakened, pained, and by now good and scared. I wobbled across the bathroom like a drunken fraternity pledge, grabbing the sink for support. Boy, some flu, I thought—the throat virus has landed in the inner ear, I figured, and upended my equilibrium. I'd better get back to the sack and stay there.

It took me another three or four minutes to navigate the fifteen or twenty feet to the bed, reeling and lurching the whole way. I made it back and lay there for a few minutes, almost in shock. The initial pain and irritation were long gone. Now I felt something much stronger: a diminution of movement. The problem during the trip across the bedroom was not just a lack of balance, it was that I couldn't pick my legs up and put them down without the effort it would take a normal person to walk through a vat of molasses. I still had feeling in my legs—if I pinched one, it hurt—but any motor response was slipping fast. Getting a leg from floor to bed was like picking up a thirty-pound deadweight, an experience that was soon to become as ordinary as sitting in a rolling chair. At the time, it felt like a slow death, from the soles of the feet upward.

Two more minutes and I decided more aspirin and more movement, more precious movement. I got up, hands on the bureau, and I flopped to the ground. I was now in a complete state of panic. My entire lower body had turned into a soft, unresponsive mass.

I crawled to the phone and called the doctor back. A half a dozen words out of my mouth, he ordered me to call 911. I did as told, still entertaining the belief that I was making way too much of this and, boy, would this be embarrassing if it turned out that I was just dizzy and weak from the flu. I called Ann-Marie at her dentist, and the dentist didn't think I was overreacting. It was in my voice.

From that first tingling in bed to calling 911 was an hour and a half. Sudden onset, they call it.

Our eight-year-old son, Max, arrived home from playing after-school basketball to hear my shouting. He located Ann-Marie's eighty-five-year-old Swedish mother, Agda, who lived with us at the time. She helped me get some pants on just as two paramedics from the fire department burst in, ready for cardiac intervention. They were beefy action-hero types in clean, starched uniforms. My rescuers, so to speak, saw me lying there, crying but cogent, quickly assessed the situation, and essentially laughed in my face. They thought I was just trying to BS my way into a free ride to the hospital.

Imagine Hans and Frans, the dumb weight lifters from *Saturday Night Live*. Crossing their massive arms and dropping their portable defibrillator, their collective on-site demeanor went from "We're in charge here!" to "What the holy heck is this?" This was not part of their training—a grown man in bed with weak legs. "This must be, like, a not very sick person," all four brain cells discharged at once. "This must be a phony baloney!"

On top of being instantly paralyzed, I was now being dissed and demeaned. They thought I was having a panic attack or maybe a muscle spasm that any fool could walk off. I wasn't comatose or writhing in pain. I wasn't calling out to God or turning blue from oxygen deprivation, so to Ponch and Larry, I must be faking it, a whiner, a hypochondriac, a girly-man. I had no idea what was going on. I could barely describe the symptoms, let alone defend myself against their stony stares. I was still holding the phone when they arrived, trying to explain the situation to Ann-Marie. In tears, I told her I couldn't move my legs or feet. "Yes, you can!" Ponch shouted out like a playground fourth-grader. "You can move your toes. I saw them move!"

Then Larry started lecturing me. "Hey, you know while we stand here talking to you, man, some old guy is probably dying of a cardiac seizure, man, someone who really needs us, so, hey, don't waste our time, okay. . . ." They then beckoned me to get up so that they could help me down the stairs. They figured Ann-Marie could take me to the hospital. They had more important things to do.

I tried to stand and again fell to the floor, whimpering. If I was faking it, I was doing an award-winning job. They had no choice but to take over. By the time they carried me down the steps like a 180-pound Baby Huey, my sense of self, fragile as it was, had vanished like the wind. This wasn't like being in a nasty car wreck or breaking your leg and being helped off the ski slope. It was closer to an acid trip—everything was warped and screwy. "There must be some way out of here, said the joker to the thief."

Max stood to the side and watched all this in silence. He kept saying, "Don't worry, Dad, you'll be fine," but he was clearly as traumatized as I was. His recollection was that I was as scared as he'd ever seen me. "It's like when I wake you after a nap nowadays," he described it, "and you don't know where you are—you had a weird, astonished, dazed look, your eyes wide open and your mouth slightly open." Ann-Marie, her mouth bloated with Novocain, arrived just as they were wheeling me out the door. She confirmed that my eyes were "wide and terrified."

The rescue unit loaded me into their ambulance and dropped me off at the nearest emergency room, at the now defunct Century City Hospital, saying no more than, "Something's wrong with his legs or something." Ann-Marie followed. My last trip to the hospital, at age fifteen, had been for a burst appendix that ruined my high school football career. This trip had every prospect of ruining my life.

The greatest fear among the attending ER staff was of what is known as an "ascending" neurological disorder: that is, one that ascends up the body and cuts off nerve response to the heart or lungs and thus induces cardiac or respiratory arrest. Guillain-Barré syndrome, which is something like polio, tends to do this. Another possibility was some kind of stroke. Now, that's a word that will send chills down your spine even when you can't feel your spine. Or it could be a "presentation," in doctor talk, that signals the onset of MS, or ALS (Lou Gehrig's Disease), or God knows what.

I remember lying on that steel slab in the ER for an interminable period of time, waiting for something else to happen. My own doctor was on his way, and the staff didn't really know what to do in the absence of some diagnosis that none of them was prepared or qualified to give. I was in no pain and, really, no discomfort, just the numb, creepy, impotent feeling of not being able to move my legs or wiggle my toes. I knew that if I went into cardiac or pulmonary arrest, these people could handle it. No horrible images of death or disease floated around my head. If the bottom half of my body weren't just lying there like a lifeless bag of flesh, I would have felt fine.

Ann-Marie was containing her own panic by calling doctors and friends as I watched paramedics wheel in a gardener who had apparently fallen from a ladder and driven some pruning shears into the base of his skull. I turned my head to check him out. He was in obvious pain but cogent enough to talk to his fellow workers as the staff prepared to move him into an operating room. This scene triggered a flashback to the only other extreme physical trauma of my life: at age fourteen, while I was trying to paint the high reaches of a two-story garage by myself, the ladder slipped and I came crashing down onto the driveway, breaking my leg and turning my left wrist into the letter U. I can't remember the pain, just looking at the wrist and wondering if it would ever work again. Everything healed up nicely, but that accident cost me another year of football. I should have taken the hint and switched to golf.

Lying beside that workman with the fractured skull, I had my first emotional epiphany of this long, strange paralytic trip. His broken head reminded me of another broken head, the principal event that had defined my life up to this point. It was my father's head, Ralph W. Rucker, M.D., age thirty-seven. And the fracture had killed him.

This family tragedy occurred when I was a little over two years old, living with my parents; two older sisters, Louise and Rosalind; and one older brother, Ralph, Jr., in a big two-story white frame house in the small oil town of Bartlesville, Oklahoma. The year was 1948. The Good War was over; my parents had survived with this picture-book family; and my father, a doctor (ear, eye, nose, and throat specialist), was just starting to build a practice in a town flush with oil money. Life looked good.

His death occurred in the middle of a freezing cold night in January—2:30 a.m., according to the local newspaper. There was a small electrical fire in the basement, probably caused by a hand iron that had been left on by mistake. As the story goes—a story that took on the force of a Greek legend by the time I was six or seven, and like such a legend, has more than one version—we were all aroused by the smoke, and my mother and father quickly called the fire department and hustled us next door to the neighbors. The firemen came and extinguished the blaze quickly. It was not much of a fire. It never left the basement.

Relieved, my father, a big, hearty guy, hauled us kids back to the house one by one and put us back in bed. He then returned to the neighbors to thank them for their kindness. As he came up the brick front steps of our house for the last time, he apparently slipped on the icy surface, fell backward, and hit his head on the edge of a step. It was a hard fall. He got up, clearly dazed by the blow. My mother wanted him to go to the hospital and get looked at immediately, but my father said no, he'd go in the morning. He would live, he said. She helped him to bed.

He fell asleep beside her that night and never woke up. He died in his sleep from a massive brain contusion. One of the local funeral parlor owners, Arnold Moore, still alive today, drove the hearse-cum-ambulance that early morning. He confirms that when he pulled up to our house, my father was dead.

It was an awful, awful thing. My father had just celebrated his thirty-seventh birthday. My mother, a thirty-six-year-old housewife, was left alone with four children, ages two through nine; no ready means of support; no life insurance; and a life irreparably damaged. She had plenty of Oklahoma relatives to help her out, but essentially she was alone in the big house with her four small children. She must have felt a stunning sense of loss. Even if my father had gotten to the local hospital while he was still alive, the staff probably couldn't have saved him. If it was an intracerebral hemorrhage—as my brother, who is now himself a doctor, assumes (there was no autopsy)—they couldn't have done a thing.

My mother never remarried and spent the next twenty years raising her children by herself. She had briefly attended medical school before meeting my father, but at the time of his death she had no marketable skills. She started her life again by going to a local typing school. This was the 1940s and 1950s, not 2006. Careers for women just didn't exist, certainly not in small, hidebound Bartlesville, Oklahoma.

She succeeded, first with the family, then with the career. She went to Little League games and Girl Scout meetings and father-and-son pancake breakfasts and nudged and nurtured her kids into adulthood. She then went back to college at age fifty-four to earn a master's degree in library science. She finished her professional life as the assistant librarian at the University of Oklahoma Medical School. Through a fierce will, she had invented a life for herself and spawned, at last count, a prosperous clan that now includes twelve grandchildren and eighteen great-grandchildren.

As I closed my eyes and lay quietly on that table in the ER, reimagining the details of my father's death, a strange thing happened, which I immediately mentioned to Ann-Marie. I felt a sense of relief, as if a long-buried emotional burden had been lifted off me. A subliminal culpability I had always felt about his accident seemed to evaporate. Somehow, some way, I had felt that his death was my fault. I think a psychiatrist had once mentioned this possibility, but I didn't buy it at the time and certainly hadn't felt any emotional change take place when he said it. Now I did.

I have no memory of my father. To this day I don't know much about him, in the sense of knowing his voice, his manner, his tics, or his view of the world. He was more of an icon in my life than a flesh-and-blood person. My mother adored him and never ceased to be married to him. A large oil painting of him, the kind you see of bank presidents and CEOs, hung prominently over the mantel in our home in Oklahoma during my entire childhood. My grandmother—an artist and art teacher—had painted the portrait from a photograph after he died and it never left my mother's view from the day it was hung until the day she died fifty-six years later. My sister Louise recalls that I once said that I was twelve before I realized that it wasn't a portrait of God.

Anyway, I now felt released from the guilt. Of course this raises a question: what did I have to feel guilty about in the first place? I had been two years old at the time—how guilty could I have been? I wasn't a devil boy; I didn't put a hex on my father. I didn't push the man down the steps or light the fire in the basement. Nevertheless, Dr. Freud, I had felt guilty—you can fill in your own four-page analysis here—and now I didn't. The sensation of relief was very strong, and amid all the fear and uncertainty of the moment it was oddly comforting.

I'm sure that by this point, Ann-Marie was also thinking of my father's accident and the emotional devastation it had wrought on my entire family, especially my mother. Ann-Marie had spent years as a working artist and fabric designer, but on that day in 1996, she was professionally afloat, filling in as a teaching assistant at our youngest son's elementary school. The main means of family support—for two kids, a private college tuition, an elderly mother, and a mortgage the size of Wisconsin—was lying on a gurney in the ER. If I died from whatever was attacking my nervous system, Ann-

Marie would be overwhelmed with responsibility. If I became permanently bedridden or brain-damaged, her fate would be even worse. Before my father died in his sleep, my mother never had time to consider what might happen. Ann-Marie had nothing but time. At that point, who the hell knew?

Blaine, away at Washington University in St. Louis, remembers getting the call. "When my mom called to break the bad news, I immediately sensed complete collapse in her voice. Nothing of this magnitude had ever affected our family." At 1,500 miles away, he couldn't quite process it. "I'd say I took the news pretty lightly. I was alone in my apartment without a live shoulder to cry on. It took me weeks to put it all into context."

Lucky kid. It took me years.

Waiting for the arrival of someone who knew what they were doing, I kept trying to puncture my fear. "This must be God's way," I announced to Ann-Marie, "of punishing me for telling too many Christopher Reeve jokes." We couldn't help laughing. We had spent the last six years in a state of unrelenting professional and financial panic. The wolf never left the door. Through a deft combination of bad luck, bad timing, a sideways career path, and rank stupidity, we had managed to create our own air-conditioned nightmare in sunny Los Angeles.

It had gotten to the point of being silly. On one Thursday afternoon, after a couple of late payments, the trusty mortgage company sent a guy in a gray sedan around to make sure we weren't smoking crack and spray-painting the walls. He made Ann-Marie sign an affidavit that we were in fact the rightful owners of the property and not some homeless gypsy squatters. In the midst of the Great California Real Estate Bust of the early 1990s, we were so desperate that we were a signature away from unloading our house for $200,000 less than we had paid for it. I sat in my little writing studio for days on end, hustling monkey work and wondering where I'd made a wrong turn. Ann-Marie cried herself to sleep night after night. We owed money to the IRS, Citibank Visa, Washington University, the Wilshire Credit Corporation, the family, and fourteen other people. And after years of uncertainty, we thought we had stuck it out, weathered the storm, seen the light at the end of the dark tunnel of a hundred strokes of bad luck and stupid life decisions. And the big payoff?

"Congratulations, Mr. and Mrs. Rucker, you made it through the hard years, and now here's your prize—a sudden, capricious, debilitating, possibly life-threatening disease that we don't even have a name for!"

Help came in the form of neurologist Dr. Daniel Rovner. Sent by my internist, he walked in, poked around for a few minutes, and then gave this catastrophe a name: transverse myelitis (TM). "Myelitis" is a nonspecific term for inflammation of the spinal cord. "Transverse" refers to the particular point on the spinal cord where the inflammation occurs. The whole spinal cord doesn't become inflamed, just a certain area. The impairment caused by this inflammation reflects the level of damage done at this one juncture.

None of this made much sense, initially, but it certainly was a starting point. First, TM is very rare. According to experts, there are one to four new cases a year per 1 million people. Another source I later read said there were something like 33,000 diagnosed cases in America around the time I

became case number 33,001. Apparently TM can affect anyone of any demographic, ethnicity, or age group. In the vast
majority of cases, it happens only once, a situation described
in medicine as uniphasal. I was happy to hear that it didn't
happen weekly.

The problem with TM is that it involves the complex bodily
mechanisms of both the immune system and the central nervous system and presents itself in a dizzying array of forms.
There is no single cause, and there is no predictable outcome.
One source of the inflammation could be a viral infection that
invades the spine, causing your immune system to go on red
alert, develop a quick-response brigade of antibodies, and inflame the area to kill the virus. This infection could be caused
by such viruses as rubella (German measles), measles, mono-
nucleosis, flu, chicken pox, or some form of hepatitis. TM has
also been associated with underlying autoimmune disorders
like MS, lupus, and sarcoidosis. According to Dr. Rovner, if
it's a virus, it's usually one occurring in the upper respiratory
or gastrointestinal area. Why such a bug would then move
to the spine and cause all this havoc, no one knows for sure.
And it's usually long gone from your system before the initial
inflammation occurs.

Or it might not be a virus at all, at least directly. It might
just be something that looks like a virus, something that met-
abolically mirrors the makeup of a virus, a faux-viral protein.
This process is known as molecular mimicry. The immune
system spots what it thinks is a foreign agent, can't tell the
difference between the real thing and the mimic, and sends
in the same death squad. Something, Lord knows what, stim-
ulates or triggers your system to inflame and damage your
spine. Is this an immune system screwup? Is there a genetic

component? Whatever the cause, the infected area of nerve cells is completely cooked by the time anyone knows what's going on. When did I know my nerve cells were dying? When I started walking around the bedroom like a wino on payday.

When the cause of a disorder like transverse myelitis is unknown or unclear, the medical term used to describe it is "idiopathic" or "of idiopathic origins." According to one web-site (Johns Hopkins), perhaps 60 percent of cases of acute non-compression myelopathy (a spinal disorder in which the spine wasn't squashed in some way) are idiopathic in origin. And that group, it later turned out, included me.

The origins of my particular condition may be unknown, but I came to learn that the circumstances surrounding my attack were not unique. At the excellent website of the Transverse Myelitis Association, www.myelitis.org, I read other first-person stories that seemed to fit a pattern. The person would have flulike symptoms around the same time as the first signs of TM, as I did; and then over a short period of time would start to feel weird nerve sensations, then an excruciating pain, then the onset of paralysis. The flulike symptoms might show up anywhere from a few hours to a few weeks before the attack. According to the website, approximately one-third of patients with TM had some kind of flulike illness going in, though there is no way they could have predicted that it would lead to something as extreme as paralysis.

The biggest problem in all this is that the nerve cells of the central nervous system—the brain and the spinal column—do not regenerate. Your spine doesn't have the biological equipment to fix itself. That is why stem cell research is so vital to those with spinal cord injuries; stem cells may be a way to grow new nerve cells to replace the ones destroyed by the inflammation or injury. You can cut off the tip of your finger or your left foot, have a doctor sew it back on, and soon the feeling will return. Iowa farmers operating heavy machinery have this done all the time. Not so when you break or damage a nerve connection in your spine. Not only is this bad news for a poor sap like me; it doesn't seem to make evolutionary sense. You can function without a thumb or a toe, or the tip of your nose, or a hundred other areas of the body where nerves regenerate. But your survival is seriously compromised when you break your back or get conked repeatedly in the brain area. Common sense would say, "Save the spine; forget the pinkie." Reality says, "Forget about walking, bud; but, hey, you can still play 'Chopsticks.'"

The good news, Dr. Rovner told us in that initial conversation, is that this condition is very unlikely to ascend into the lungs, heart, or brain and is thus not explicitly life-threatening. In most incidents, it doesn't progress and doesn't recur. The really good news, he went on, is that in many cases the condition reverses itself. The nerve damage can be partial or temporary. After the inflammation subsides, the picture changes and some nerve function or sensation returns. The common medical wisdom is that in about one-third of patients in my situation, there is recovery with minimal long-term effects. In another third, there is a return of some function: maybe developing enough function in the legs to go from a wheelchair to crutches or a walker. In the final third, nothing happens—there is no reversal, no return of function, no wiggling of the big toe, nothing. The person remains as paralyzed as he or she was when the inflammation first presented itself.

This information instantly cheered us up. We were elated to know that, A, I wasn't going to die from this, at least not directly; and B, with any luck, I'd walk again, either with or without a zippy-looking handmade Highlands walking stick. Hey, I said to myself, I was in the top one-third on my high school SAT scores. Surely I can do as well on the SAT of life.

It was only after an exhaustive battery of late-night tests that the doctors could be sure of this diagnosis. I was moved to Cedars-Sinai Medical Center in Los Angeles, soon to become my home away from home, and was subjected to hours of medical unpleasantries. "Spinal Tap," for you young people out there, is not just the name of the world's greatest faux rock band. It is a dangerous and excruciatingly painful extraction of spinal fluid used to diagnose neurological disorders like MS, or at least it was in 1996. The needle used is like something out of a Mel Brooks movie. It's unfortunate that they had to insert it in the part of my spine that I could still feel.

The staff at Cedars-Sinai also tried a massive injection of steroids to counteract the inflammation and perhaps mitigate the damage to the nerve cells in that area. That didn't last long. I had a violent reaction to the steroids—I thought my heart had stopped—so they were quickly stopped. That was the one attempt at intervention, and it sadly failed.

After a couple of days of waiting and watching for some other weirdness to occur, I was finally moved to a long stay on the seventh-floor rehabilitation wing. Stage one—sudden onset and stabilizing the freaked-out patient—was over. Stage two—the patient gets used to his new condition and relearns stuff he thought he had mastered as a toddler—was next. I was in shock and at a complete loss to comprehend what had just happened to me. Every night of that first week in rehab,

I dreamed about what had occurred on that Tuesday afternoon between 1:00 and 2:30. I tried to recollect every precious moment of that downward spiral, from the initial pain to the discomfort to wobbling and lurching across the bedroom, over and over again, like a person desperate to stay on his feet for as long as possible. I now see that in those dreams, I was trying to preserve the memory of walking, since, as it sadly evolved, that was the last time I would ever have the pleasure.

TWO

PARALYZED LIKE ME

I SPENT THE NEXT SEVEN weeks in the hospital, learning to reprogram my life around this horrible impairment. The idea that I would actually have to function as a paralytic was terrifying. Just sitting on the edge of the hospital bed for the first time, held up by a nurse so I wouldn't flop over, was terrifying. Being lifted for the first time into a reclining wheelchair was terrifying. Coming to terms with my skinny friend the urinary catheter was terrifying. It was all terrifying.

I had a profound sense that my life was starting over or at least going into some dark phase of withdrawal and reentry. On top of the fear, I seemed to be waiting for something—if not for more epiphanies like the one about my father, at least for the paralysis to go away so I could get back to living. I even started numbering the days, the way a network news show would hype an international hostage crisis—"AR Held Hostage, Day 4." I was hoping that someone somewhere was negotiating my release.

Even with the demands of physical and occupational therapy—from Wheelchair 101 to toilet training—there's not much to do in a hospital. On Day 33, for instance, well into my incarceration, I wrote: "Staying in the hospital puts you in the present. You no longer mourn the past or fear the future. You only fear lunch."

I settled into a room in the rehab ward and was inundated with the succor of a hundred friends. My older brother, Ralph, a retired neonatologist, flew out from Haskell, Oklahoma, to ask all the right questions and serve as the family ombudsman. He had become a gentleman cattle rancher after his career in medicine, and he has a formidable Okie presence. It was very comforting to have him around. Blaine rushed home from college. In his words, "I hopped on a plane to LA, walked down the gallery-like walls of Cedars, and finally got my long-awaited visual confirmation. It wasn't my dad's red running shoes. It was my old man laid up in a hospital bed. My first thought was: he is dying."

Others weighed in with disbelief and jokes. One friend, Harry Shearer, took the Shirley MacLaine approach: "Boy, you must have really f**ked someone over in a past life." A writer friend called to work out the beats of the potential TV-movie pitch. "Look at me, Doc! I'm a broken man. I can't dance with Concetta or play soccer with little Al. Not to mention figure skating." My high school pal Bill King sent me a different weird special-interest magazine every three days, cult favorites like *Submachine Gun Monthly*, *Modern Cheerleading*, and *Tattooing Today*. It was an ingenious way to raise my spirits.

As some friends checked in daily with deli sandwiches, the complete films of Alfred Hitchcock, or just kindness, others were curiously absent. It was my first indication that my new condition could breed fear in people other than myself. "Criptophobics," you could call them. Or maybe they were just hospital-o-phobics. Thank God I was going to be like this for only a short time, I thought.

I figured I would have six to nine months of impairment and then, given my heavily reinforced chin-up attitude and general state of good health, I'd start down the slow path to renewed mobility. I even started a book in my head called *Paralyzed Like Me*, inspired by one of my favorite books when I was in high school, the classic sociological study *Black Like Me*. If this wasn't on your required reading list, it's the story of an enterprising southern reporter, John Howard Griffin, who had his skin pigment darkened to brown to experience racism firsthand. The book predated the big civil rights push of the 1960s and left an indelible impression on my fifteen-year-old conscience.

In my own presumably temporary paralysis, I thought, I had been given this huge bay window into the everyday world of the disabled—the fear, the hassles, the humiliation, and the inevitable insults to come—and once I was walking again, I could relate my experience without pity or rancor. I would have, to put it crudely, "crip creds." I could become a champion of the disabled without actually having to live as one. I was merely a disabled person in residence.

When Dr. Rovner guaranteed that I would end up "somewhere between FDR and perfect," I heard "perfect." I might not ever run another 10K race, but I would certainly dance again with Concetta.

At least my waking mind heard "perfect." My dream mind apparently never got the memo that I was paralyzed at all. Like most paralyzed people, or so I've heard, I have never dreamed of myself in a wheelchair or on crutches or using a walker. I sometimes walk oddly in my dreams, as if I've just stood up after a long sitting spell and my legs are a little numb and wobbly. Sometimes I walk very slowly and carefully, as if crossing an icy pond. I've even said to other people in a dream, "Listen, let's get something straight. This is just a dream, you know. In real life I can't walk a lick." They usually smile and wink. But I'm never paralyzed, not even in nightmares. If I'm being chased by some sinister Other down a long, dark alley, I'm running like a Kenyan marathoner. If I'm making love, all systems are go, if you catch my drift.

I'm no Carl Jung, but what this shows me is that I've never really accepted the fact that I am paralyzed. Or maybe I know full well that I am, but I have subconsciously concluded, "Why harp about it in your sleep? You're just making this stuff up, you know—walk, run, dance like Baryshnikov, who the hell cares?" If, in Mark Twain's quip, a game of golf is just a good walk ruined, then paralysis is just a good dream ruined.

In the hospital, this waking/dreaming dichotomy was painful. There was one recurring, almost nightly dream of escape. I'd see myself outside the Cedars complex in the middle of the night, crossing a big street, San Vicente Boulevard, stealing toward home. I am slinking down low, so that no one will see me, but I'm happy. Boy, will Ann-Marie be surprised when I walk in the door, I'm thinking. My only problem is getting across San Vicente. Once that's accomplished, I'm home free.

As you can probably guess, I never make it across that street. Invariably, halfway through the effort, I'd wake up to see if the paralysis had suddenly remitted and walking home was even a vague possibility. I'd reach down under the sheets and pinch or slap my leg, hard. Nothing. This was always a blow. It got to the point that I dreaded going to sleep because I dreaded waking up and feeling my dead legs. Alone, in the dark, in my hospital bed—that's when I really knew what was going on. That's when the true sadness began.

Not that I slept much anyway. For weeks, I didn't know how to sleep. Sleeping on my back, arms at my side, like Dracula in his coffin, seemed the easiest way, but paralytics need to shift body position every two hours to avoid the dreaded bedsore. That's all the time it takes for the skin to break down in a paralyzed area and a sore to appear, a sore that will take months to heal, assuming it doesn't become infected and lead to worse problems. As I wrote to myself on Day 23 of the hostage crisis, I have three sleeping choices: staring at the ceiling, staring at the door, and staring at the bathroom door. It took me years to get used to setting an alarm and turning like a rotisseried chicken three or four times a night. However smoothly you master this, your sleep is pretty much interrupted for life.

Waking up in the morning continues to be the worst time of day for someone who is paralyzed. The shift between lying down like any other sleeper and then opening your eyes to survey the damage anew each day is the very definition of a rude awakening. An hour later you're doing whatever you do, but for those first few minutes you are newly paralyzed all over again. It's a daily mental adjustment, and it's always a drag. Halfway through your morning get-out-of-bed ritual—

in my case, removing a whole array of devices to keep me free of pressure sores during the night—you just want to fall back and say, "Screw this. I'm calling in sick."

In those early days, at the same time I was banking on the prospect of a remission, I was also beginning to mourn the loss of half of my body. I didn't know it at the time, but that was what I was doing—kissing a good part of my old self, and my old life, good-bye. I had absolutely no sense of the future, but I was pretty sure I wouldn't be wearing my de rigueur mid-twenties costume of steel-tipped cowboy boots and tight blue jeans again in this lifetime. Or getting up at five in the morning and running five miles around the Hollywood reservoir. Even the idea of leaving my hospital room was scary enough. Perhaps the saddest loss of all was the knowledge that one thing which had been a healthy concern, if not an unhealthy obsession, since the age of twelve—sex—was now fading like a mirage in the desert. I could just feel it. Or not feel it, as the case may be.

I remember tuning in to an episode of *NYPD Blue* on the hospital TV one night. It opened with a lithe female body stepping into or out of a steamy shower, then wrapping her legs around a half-dressed Jimmy Smits. I watched for a few minutes, then shouted at the TV, "Hey, where's the damn crime plot here? When are you going to arrest someone? Or is the whole show just about *this*?"

With all the bad feelings going through my head—fear, guilt, loss, more fear—I began to see the hospital more as a sanctuary than a prison. Except when the occupational or physical therapists forced me to, I didn't really have to leave my bed. It was my little bomb shelter of sanity, my own raft down the Mississippi. I had total access to E-mail and the

Internet, books, the *Jerry Springer Show*, the Beatles on CDs (this was pre-iPod), and the latest edition of *Outlaw Biker* or *Steel Horse Rider* full of bare-breasted biker chicks. I had all day, every day, to indulge my sedentary side.

The staff brought me food and medicine; friends brought me more food; I could watch old George Burns and Gracie Allen shows on one of the in-house hospital channels; and some of the nurses, in the sappiest of clichés, became like Madonna figures to me. They were kindness personified. One beautiful night nurse thought it was her God-ordained mission to bring solace and care to patients like me. Even though we were both happily married, in one drug-induced moment of weakness I actually proposed to her. It was the Stockholm syndrome for sick people.

Once I learned to get around in a wheelchair, if I got really, really bored I could, with assistance, climb into the chair late at night and slowly wheel up and down the hallways of this gigantic hospital. With no one around and the walls of Cedars covered with first-rate artwork donated by wealthy patrons, it was more like tooling around the Guggenheim or a monastery than a depository of the sick. And deadly quiet.

I came to feel so comfortable in that hospital that I feared I was developing a strange case of Munchausen Syndrome by Paralysis. Munchausen syndrome is a mental condition in which people fabricate being sick and often end up making themselves sick just for the sake of attention. I wasn't pretending to be sick, but I was definitely getting into *being* sick. I looked up Munchausen on the Internet, and according to one site, "Munchausenites" had "problems with their identity, intense feelings, inadequate impulse control, a deficient sense of reality, and brief psychotic episodes." Lying in my hospital bed, crying uncontrollably, incontinent, thinking the night nurse was the Madonna, I was sure this site was talking about me!

For a long time after that first hospital stay, I would catch myself wanting to go back into Cedars for a few days so that the staff could run a few tests, take my temperature every fifteen minutes, and keep track of some pesky pressure wound. Cedars was safe, clean, and familiar; the world outside was dangerous and alien. No one at Cedars would let me fall off my chair and hit the ground while trying to transfer from the car; or if such a thing did happen on the hospital grounds, six orderlies would be there to pick me up. No one at Cedars would look at me strangely or convey in some subtle fashion that I was odd, pathetic, repulsive, or even impaired. There were patients at Cedars a lot sicker than I—I was one of the healthier ones, all things considered. I wasn't in terrible pain, I wasn't delirious, and I wasn't dying. I had my needs, and they fulfilled every one of them at the beep of a call button. Why would I want to leave?

My room was in the middle of a stroke ward, and with one or two exceptions, I was the youngest whippersnapper there. A lot of not-so-sick but troublesome oldsters in Los Angeles get dumped by rich relatives at Cedars-Sinai—"Cedars Palace," they call it—but none of these pampered semi-invalids are in the stroke ward. They're over in the Elizabeth Taylor/Frank Sinatra wing, eighth floor, North Tower, enjoying the facial wraps and sushi chefs. Stroke patients occupy another level of hell. For all my feelings of sadness and self-pity, my T-10 paralysis looked pretty darn puny compared with the ravages of a stroke. As I watched these other patients struggle to form words or pick up a toy block, my Munchausen-by-Paralysis wet dream started to fade, and I gained some perspective on degrees of impairment. Compared with the inability to speak, the inability to urinate on cue was laughably insignificant.

Before I began to wheel around the hospital nightly, it was a very big deal for me to leave my room. The first time I could power myself down the hall in a wheelchair was a real thrill. It sounds stupid—I mean, who can't operate a wheelchair?—but I was scared of everything at this point. I decided one day to take my lunch in the sunroom at the end of the corridor. So I grabbed my stale tuna sandwich on white bread and chips and wheeled down to this airy room, from which you could see the whole city. As I entered, I realized it was filling up with stroke patients, a combination group outing and practical occasion to work on the simplest skills like buttering bread or sipping soup. As I found my place at a back table, I discovered more patients coming in and blocking my exit. I was stuck.

The patients next to me were very kind, less outwardly freakish or deformed than I was, and happy to see me. They wanted to communicate with me in the simplest way—on the level of "Nice day, isn't it?" or "I don't trust the tuna here"—but they couldn't. Their mouths didn't work; their speech was indecipherable, at least to me. I kept leaning in, trying to catch a passing word. By the look on my face, they knew I wasn't getting it. This frustrated them all the more, so they spoke louder. They were shouting to be understood, and I was deeply embarrassed. I didn't know how to respond. One aneurysm ago, I kept thinking, they were perfectly cogent. One unstable piece of arterial plaque floating up their bloodstream had transformed them from normal into incomprehensible. I kept nodding and smiling and looking into their eyes. All I could see was fear and confusion. If it was a nightmare for me, imagine what it was like for them.

Finally, one of the nurses saw me struggling and failing to interact and kindly wheeled me out of the room. She could see that, in my tender state, I was overwhelmed. I guess it was the tears that gave me away.

Everything, in those early days, was an occasion for crying. I was messed up, man. I had been brought down hard and frankly didn't know if I had the capacity to deal with it. I played along like a trouper but I certainly didn't feel like one. Visitors kept saying that I was clearly doing better, holding up better, than they would in the same situation. Of course, they didn't really know, since none of them had ever been in such a situation. And in my own mind, I was a bit of a poseur—I wasn't really holding up all that well. I tried to keep up the tomfoolery and the isn't-this-weird attitude during visiting hours and saved the heavy, uncontrollable, out-loud sobbing and hysterics for after hours. In the middle of the night. Every night.

The truth is, I've never cried so much in my life. Initially I would break down three or four times a day, completely out of the blue, in short, staccato spurts. I came to see it as an undercurrent of sadness, like an underground reservoir I didn't know existed. The paralysis was like a crack in the bedrock. It would usually be a full-blown, uncontrollable spasm lasting two or three minutes. And it would always be an enormous relief.

I got out a lot more grief in those crying jags than just the grief of not walking. I figured that I emptied a surprisingly deep grief well. Whatever else had saddened me in the previous fifty-one years of life, from my father's disappearance when I was two years old to buckteeth when I was eight to crippling anxiety and panic attacks when I was in high school and college to multiple embarrassments and failures in adulthood, I cried right out of me. I have no idea if this makes any psychoanalytical sense; it made plenty of sense to me at the time, and still does. I was cleaning house.

If dreams provided a place for me to walk around and feel human, they also were the channel of abject fear. Because I wasn't paralyzed in dreamland, paralysis couldn't be the direct source of the terror. One recurring ambulatory dream haunts me to this day. I'm standing outside my house in a dense fog, and I see a cold, murderous male face—black beard, black eyes. It quickly fades back into the haze. I try to yell a warning to Ann-Marie and the kids, but nothing comes out of my mouth. I grab a leg of a table, ready to bash heads, but suddenly my vision is dim and blurry. Then I see two murderous faces. If I go for one, the other goes for me. And they move quickly. And I can't quite see them. And I can't scream. You get the idea. I'm sure it's a textbook nightmare about vulnerability and helplessness, but it scared the bejesus out of me.

The crying and the dreams were pretty much out of my control, like most things in those early days. Only later did I figure out what was going on subconsciously. At fifty-one, I had returned to the status of an infant. I was back to square one, somewhere between the delivery room and potty training. And since the hospital food tasted pretty much like pabulum, it was a total sensory experience.

From moment one, I couldn't move. Even as a paraplegic, with half of my body still normal, I initially had no idea how to manipulate my limbs. I was helpless. A nurse had to come and flip me on my side twice a night to prevent skin breaks. I had no full-body motor skills. I was like a fish flapping on the beach.

Have you ever seen a wheelchair basketball player fall over while charging the basket, then almost miraculously flip himself back up on his wheels and keep going? Try it sometime. It's an advanced athletic skill, more difficult, no doubt, than balancing on a high beam or hitting a golf ball straight. Now imagine a six-month-old baby doing that. Now imagine me as that baby.

I'd sit up; I'd fall over. If the staff didn't put up guardrails, I'd move to turn and fall out of bed. The distance between my body and the wheelchair at the side of the bed was an abyss. How was I going to get from here to there? That might sound silly to you walkers, but it is scary business for the newly paralyzed to sit in a wheelchair. It makes plain just how impaired you are.

In other words, the shift was not just psychological. It was an observable fact. Physically, I had gone from competence to incompetence, not to mention from continent to incontinent. I was incapable of many of the most rudimentary human skills, things I had pretty much mastered by the age of three. Talk about regression therapy. I didn't have to pretend to be a baby. In many ways, I was one.

I'm a near-total T-10 paralytic. That means I have no nerve function from about the waist down. That in turn means I have no control of my bladder, my colon, or any other body part down there. And no feeling. Practically speaking, this is not a big deal—thousands of otherwise normal Americans live and function like this every day—but it takes a little getting used to, dignity-wise.

First, you must wear "adult undergarments." A clue to the embarrassment this engenders is the frequency with which it comes up as a joke line among off-color comedians from Redd Foxx to *The Man Show*. It's right up there in standard outré humor with flatulence, colostomy bags, and penile enlargement. Ever since Depends starting running commercials, some aspiring "Club Yuk-Yuk" stand-up somewhere has tried to make an audience cringe with his "edgy" adult diaper material.

"You know, my grandpa now has to wear those Depends things, like you see on TV. . . . How many people in the audience wear those things? (Audience titters.) . . . You know, no one has ever raised their hand. I wonder why. . . . (Big laugh.) . . . I think Gramps buys used ones, probably on eBay. . . . Actually, he calls them 'previously owned'—one owner only, he promises me. . . . (Audience groans.) . . . But, man, he should check the mileage of those things, because, whew, that smelly old codger can empty a mall. . . . (Comedian speaks as mall security guard.) . . . It's all right, folks, no need to panic, it's not a bioterrorist stink bomb, it's just Gramps going to the drugstore. . . . (Big laugh. Then a beat.) . . . Isn't it great that old people can't smell, especially themselves. . . . Unfortunately, the rest of us . . ."

For all of you aging baby boomers with bladder management problems on the horizon, you'll be happy to hear that they now make these security garments in all kinds of appealing, worry-free shapes and sizes. Soon there will probably be designer ones by Calvin Klein or Ralph Lauren (in a rugged,

Wyoming rancher motif), advertised in *Vanity Fair*. Just be prepared, at least early on, to face a three-changes-a-day blow to your dignity. And get someone else to buy them for you at the drugstore. They are impossible to hide behind a *National Enquirer*, and you shouldn't have to face that smirky double take from the bag boy.

Beyond the Depends, there is initially a built-in urinary catheter—a tube to replace your atrophied bladder—that leads to a little bag on the side of the bed, which is not the first thing you want guests to see when they enter the room. Later you learn to catheterize yourself at periodic intervals during the day, and it becomes second nature. Sometimes you miss an appointment, so to speak, because you have no feeling that your bladder is full, if not overflowing, but that's another story.

It's the bowel function, or lack thereof, that is the most problematic and potentially petrifying. This is beyond coarse humor. Only Larry Flynt would look for a joke in this neighborhood. Not wanting to offend a whole group of squeamish readers, I'll tiptoe through this.

The moment of my first, ah, encounter with a paralytic bowel came about unexpectedly, as such moments usually do. I was practicing "transferring," the art of going from bed to chair and from chair to shower bench. Being a complete geek at this seemingly simplest of human tasks, I was totally engaged in the exercise. Having done a round of successful transfers, I was about to do the last one, back into bed, when all present—the nurse, the occupational therapist, my wife, and I—noticed simultaneously that I had had a distasteful "accident." A major distasteful accident.

Instantly I felt profound shame. Before, I had thought shame was doing something unseemly like passing out at a restaurant after one too many zombies or getting caught in the adolescent act by your older sister. Now I knew. That was ego-deflating. This was humiliating.

But what can you do? The professionals in the room have seen this a hundred times, and your spouse, unless he or she is abnormally fastidious, will come to accept such events as the price of paralysis. The only sane response is to clean it up and go on with the next thing and try everything in your power to see that it doesn't happen again. Which it will, in some form or another, just when you least expect it. You are ever mindful of the possibility. You are ever mindful of how unpredictable and out of control your body has become.

Though reduced to a middle-aged infant, I tried to formalize a conscious way of behaving during my waking hours. I gave myself two ironclad rules of conduct. One: Never whine. No one likes a whiner, except professional whine-catchers like therapists and rabbis. A whiner in a wheelchair is even worse. Faced with one, any sane person will obey the natural impulse to look sad, pat you on the back, and get the hell out of the room. It's a double assault—visual and auditory. You go to see a newly paralyzed friend, he starts whining about the raw deal he's been handed, and you leave feeling somehow responsible for the fact that *he* got paralyzed! Plus, no one listens anyway.

The second rule was never to ask, "Why me?" It is a stupid, unanswerable question that only invites self-pity and more whining. Or self-blame. How do I know that I didn't bring this on myself, through some self-induced malfunction triggered by years of anxiety, stress, narcissism, or single-malt

Scotch? I don't know, of course. No one knows, at least no one who's ever talked to me. Short of hard evidence to the contrary, I figure it's best to just chalk it up to bad luck. Wrong place, wrong spine. I wasn't responsible for my father's slipping on the ice and dying in his sleep when I was two, and I'm not responsible for this. Next question.

It took a while for me to arrive at this position. A mysterious ailment like this, which maybe, possibly, theoretically could be caused by something that I ate, drank, did, or didn't do, is an invitation to self-incrimination. Again, an extended stay in a hospital bed is a retreat from daily distractions, and you have a lot of downtime to ruminate about your failings. You begin to itemize to yourself all the stupid, dangerous, or egregious shit you've ever done—much of which you would never admit to anyone—and you try to find some connection between that flaw or misdeed and this punishment.

What about drugs, I wondered? I had sampled the full array of popular sixties and seventies drugs in my sordid youth, especially hallucinogens that, A, scared the hell of me and, B, probably did serious psychological if not cellular brain damage. What if the foolish ingestion of some wiggy mind-scrambler du jour—peyote buttons, for instance, or morning glory seeds laced with DDT—had caused some weird defect in my immune system? (How long had it taken scientists to discover the link between smoking and lung cancer?) As an aging baby boomer, maybe I was on the cutting edge of a whole new field of crushing, chemically induced immune system disorders.

So I laid my entire drug history out for the medical team to ponder. "Yes," I was waiting for them to announce, "it just so happens that we just found out that after a thirty-year delay,

magic mushrooms cause spinal cord inflammation and mor-
bidity. There's your answer right there." Instead, they smiled
obligingly and said there was nothing in the literature that
points to this, see you on Tuesday.

What about a sexually transmitted viral agent? What if the
trigger was some pre-AIDS, premarital, unprotected encounter with a woman as innocent of STDs as the whole country
once was? Not to mention any mindless indiscretions that
might have happened when my wife and I weren't getting
along, should they have occurred. As with the drug theory,
I again looked back to the let-loose ethos of the hippie era
and tried to attach some dire consequence to the way I had
behaved then. I was starting to think like William Bennett—
when in doubt, blame it on the 1960s.

Again, the doctors said, in one sure voice, "Not a chance."
Whatever viral or bacterial infection, if any, brought this
about, it had entered the body at most ten to twelve days
before the inflammation. It might have been the sore throat
virus I thought I had before the paralysis hit; but since that
was gone before anyone could investigate, it was a dead
end. In any case, anything from the distant past, especially
anything thirty years earlier, was out of the picture. To the
doctors this incessant hand-wringing seemed like the Jerry
Falwell "homosexuality causes AIDS" school of medicine.

Having rejected sex and drugs, I turned to my professional
frustrations. Tormented by work, I never stopped working.
For as long as I can remember, I have never allowed myself to
get sick. I'd never give in to a cold or the flu, never take that
extra day to rest up and recuperate. I was afraid that I would
miss something if I wasn't minding my workstation; or, con-
versely, I was afraid I'd be seduced by the indolent life, pull

a Brian Wilson, and never get out of bed. Again, John Calvin was at work here: only the weak get sick. If you're sick, something's wrong with your character, man. No healthy person ever gets sick.

Working through all this, I kept thinking of Susan Sontag's much-ballyhooed essay, "Illness as Metaphor." Highly simplified, her point was that illness is not a metaphor for a poor self-image, sloth, emotional frigidity, or any other moral or psychological failing. It is not a sign of the sick person's character or worldview, good or bad. It is not the wages of past sin. It is just illness.

Of course you might get lung cancer if you smoke too many cigarettes—but that's not a metaphor; it's a fact. You also might get lung cancer without smoking cigarettes. It's not because you're a bad person. It's because you have bad lungs or a flawed gene or something else beyond your control.

I bought this argument, or at least tried to buy it. Still, it was hard for me to think of a disease so profoundly life-altering as random, arbitrary, gratuitous, or "of idiopathic origin." However, that's what the experts kept telling me: we don't know exactly what happened, and for all practical purposes—i.e., your future recovery and well-being—we don't care. Actually, they soon stopped talking altogether. I'd spin another far-fetched hypothesis, and they'd give me the Blank Stare. It was clear I had reached the end of their medical curiosity, if not their medical knowledge. It was like a highway that just stops in the middle of the desert.

Still, I craved an explanation, either as a way of letting myself off the hook ("You ate a bad burrito and contracted a weird strain of salmonella poisoning") or as a way of reforming myself so that I could live a guilt-free, hopefully ambulatory life ("You got this from cannabis toxicity, and if you clean up, you'll be fine"). So I kept badgering the doctors. Tell me something, for Christ's sake, even a great big bullshit theory that I could use as a jumping-off point to plan my forward strategy.

They wouldn't budge. They stuck to their testimony like John Gotti at a double murder trial. Dr. Rovner later told me that in a situation like this—a rare, hard-to-diagnose neurological disease—the neurologist is often the only physician in the room with any clue about what's going on, and the patient leans solely on him or her for insight. Any wild guess about cause or effect could likely have one of two results: false hope or no hope. It's a murky situation, and a murky explanation is the only way to go. "Between FDR and perfect," he said, "at least establishes the image of Franklin Roosevelt, a man who found a way of conquering paralysis and achieving great things." It was a better prognosis than "between a panhandler and a shut-in."

Guilty or not, I remained a skinless chicken. On many days, I didn't want visitors, even my own family. I became completely self-absorbed, even more so than usual, if that's possible. When anyone came through the door, I had to put on a brave face and tell them how I was feeling, when I had no idea how I was feeling. I was still trying to figure that out. And until I did, I wanted to be alone, inside my own head.

It was almost a hallucinogenic state, especially when others were around. Imagine having a waking nightmare in which you are frozen in time and space while everyone else in the room is trying to figure out what to order from the deli. I wasn't angry. I wasn't even sad—at least, not between my private crying jags. I was just out there, man, like someone who'd ingested a psychoactive drug and no longer shared a consensus reality with the people he knew best. Outside I could still chat and carry on. Inside I thought someone else was doing the chatting while I was busy deciphering what was really going on.

Ann-Marie picked up on this sense of isolation right away and felt even a greater estrangement from me than she had before the crisis. I was no longer sitting alone in my studio behind the house, fretting endlessly about the future. I was now alone in a hospital room, fretting endlessly about this strange new state. Not only was I emotionally cut off; I was also useless. She still had the same family obligations as before but now got zero help from me. I couldn't even take out the trash, let alone buttress her emotionally.

Ann remembers pretty much sleepwalking through this early period. She was in shock, suspended in her own limbo between two disconnected realities. She took a long leave from teaching and tried to lose herself in the rhythm of mundane duties—buying groceries, doing laundry, going to soccer games—but it all seemed less real if not absurd after this cruel new twist. She remembers going to Max's last soccer game of the season in a kind of obligatory fog. She stood far away from the other parents, waiting for a game she couldn't care less about to be over. One woman came over and asked where I was, since I rarely missed a game. Ann blurted out the whole story, as if she couldn't wait to tell someone. When she saw the thunderstruck look on the woman's face, she broke down.

As long as only a few close friends knew, it was like a family secret. But once everyone knew, from fellow teachers to soccer moms, it became a public tragedy and all the more painful. When people are speechless in your presence, it's hard to sidestep the awful reality of things. "Paralyzed? Just like that? That's horrifying!" A chorus of such reactions only heightens your own horror.

As is often the case with people in a state of turmoil, Ann stopped eating. She remembers the momentary thrill of running to the Gap across the street from the hospital to get something to wear for the steady stream of visitors and realizing she was a full size smaller. Hey, she thought to herself, if you've got to play the beleaguered spouse, you should look your best. She called this the "major catastrophe" diet.

Like a survivor of an airline crash or a heart attack, Ann saw the world anew. Driving back from the hospital one day, she remembers stopping at a light and seeing a group of bedraggled people standing at a bus stop. You are so lucky, she thought. You have legs to stand on. And you don't even know it.

The first time I left the hospital grounds, maybe a month after I became paralyzed, Ann-Marie and a physical therapist helped me wheel myself to the big mall across the street. My first test was to power myself across the intersection at a green light. I might as well have been crossing an eight-lane freeway at rush hour, as in the Eddie Murphy highway scene in *Bowfinger*. From a sitting position, cars loomed up like monsters out of *Star Wars*, every pit in the street was an obstacle, and the other side of the street seemed half a mile away.

By arrangement, we were to meet an old friend, Paul Goldsmith, at Starbucks for coffee. You know, like normal people. I gamely pulled into the Starbucks patio, saw Paul for the first time since the incident, and broke down crying. I couldn't handle it. I was ashamed and afraid. My God, I thought, I'm a freak. I'm a pathetic freak, a cripple, one of life's sad cases. I hated that field trip. I couldn't wait to get back to the comfort and isolation of the hospital room. Munchausen City.

On that same trip to the mall, a woman pulled her kid abruptly away from my vicinity and a couple of mad shoppers pushed me out of the way so that they could beat me to the elevator. To any person in a chair out there, this is not news. To me, it was a whole new world of insults.

My principal task for most of my hospital stay was to learn the rudimentary "activities of daily living" that would allow me to function outside the place. The hospital staff called it rehabilitation, but Rovner preferred the term "habilitation"— I wasn't going to get better, just habituated to the condition. I practiced the mundane human tasks that are boring to read about but critical to, you know, living. Learning to transfer, turn over, balance on the edge of a bed, bend down, sit up, and put on a T-shirt without tumbling sideways. Learning self-catherization, or "self-cath"—bluntly, it's a matter of sticking a tube into your bladder to let the urine flow out—and other bodily functions. Learning to avoid accidents, injuries to areas you don't feel, infections, bedsores, and all the other possible complications of the paralyzed life.

A resident psychologist dropped by regularly to help in any way he could. He thought I should create an image in my mind in a state of meditation, someone or something that could provide comfort if not direction. I struggled with the meditation but did find, briefly, an "ally" in my imagination, an old farmer named Orville who lived in a farmhouse in Oklahoma that I had loved as a kid. He was in his seventies, was dressed in OshKosh B'Gosh overalls, and seldom stopped shuffling from barn to field and back. He didn't say much, except things like "Well, there you go," "It wouldn't surprise me," and "Gotta get back to work." Orville was a worker and a tight-lipped stoic. He was no poet of the prairie. He didn't ask a lot of questions or provide a lot of answers. Ask him something profound and he'd be likely to answer, "Beats me." He was no shoulder to cry on. He didn't have time for crying. I enjoyed his phlegmatic presence, but given my naturally short attention span and all the other things I was worried about, he didn't stick around long in my mind. In retrospect, he was probably a good influence and even a key to confronting my dilemma with much less hand-wringing and self-incrimination. Orville confronted reality with blithe indifference. I should have been more attuned to the old codger.

We had Christmas in my hospital room—Ann-Marie, her mother, Blaine, and Max. I loved it. Ann-Marie hated it. Maybe she had seen one too many of those happy-sad Yuletide news stories in which pro football players drop off oversize presents for kids stuck in the cancer ward. The family gave me a new bicycle helmet. I wore it in bed for a while. Maybe Ann had a premonition that I would never have a chance to wear it for real.

Max considers that Christmas in the hospital one of his favorite Christmases ever. "We took all the presents, put them in some big suitcases, and went over to Cedars-Sinai.... I got a PlayStation and a football game for PlayStation—Game

Day 96–97.... They ordered a second TV into the room and Blaine and I played that game for hours.... It was a very happy occasion.... I'll always remember that."

Kids ... they see the PlayStation, but they don't see the freaked-out paralyzed dad with the stupid bike helmet on his head. Go figure.

Max did sense the loneliness at home while I was away. "Every day was so similar," he later said. "After school, I'd go to 7-Eleven to get a hot dog and a Snickers ice cream bar, either go to the hospital or come home, and there were not a lot of people around, because Mom would usually be at the hospital. Blaine was in St. Louis and nothing much was happening.... We weren't together as a family very much."

I knew my kids would survive in the short term—their mother was clearly on the case—but I worried about what might happen to them emotionally four or five years down the road. Would they act out in some way to express their inexpressible fear or anger? Would they resent my ailment and all the attention it took away from their lives? Max seemed, at least in my presence, unfazed by the situation; I took this as denial. Blaine seemed much more shaken by it—he broke down the first time he saw me. The truth is that in my own state of self-absorption, I largely forgot about their needs. I was missing in action, and I'm sure that on some level, they suffered.

By Day 39, I was ready to get out. The insurance company had pulled the plug on my rehabilitation, and I didn't like the place enough to spend $3,000 a day to use the call button and dine on inedible sloppy joes. All things considered, I probably would have preferred to move to another, more bucolic asylum and avoid normal life for as long as I could;

but apparently Blue Cross didn't offer a long-term recovery program in Fiji.

A few days before I headed home, I got some bad news from Dr. Rovner. The latest MRI showed no appreciable reduction in the spinal swelling. None of the drugs I had been taking had lessened the inflammation or sped up the healing process. Until the swelling receded, there was no way of telling if any sensation below the point of inflammation would return. It would be at least another six months, he thought, before we would know the extent of the damage. So I wouldn't be walking out of the hospital. Again, I found this news crushing. I had known I wouldn't be walking out of the hospital, but I couldn't handle hearing it officially. I knew I'd have to go home in my new Quickie 2 wheelchair; and I also knew that living with paralysis, as opposed to being hospitalized with paralysis, would be a new source of turmoil and confusion.

Only later did I figure out what exactly was scaring me right then. In the hospital, I thought I had brought this nightmare on myself, until the doctors' Blank Stare had finally beaten me down. Now I had a new apprehension—not being able to cut it. What if I wasn't up to the task of curing myself, or at least handling the sadness and depression that were sure to come? What if I didn't have the grit and determination of the proverbial high school football player with a broken back who is up and walking on crutches in six months? What if I lacked the spiritual resources of a believer who could turn this into a new, selfless calling? What if I was too lazy or too defeatist to go from one research lab to another in search of a breakthrough?

On Day 41, I went home. The moment I wheeled myself out of Cedars and delicately plopped into Ann-Marie's Volvo,

I had another major crying jag. These weren't tears of joy and release. They were tears of fear. I was paralyzed, a cripple. I was a goddamn cripple, and now I was back in the world, no longer living in the nurturing limbo-land of the seventh floor at Cedars. This was it. And at that moment, "it" looked a lot scarier than those two murderous faces coming at me in the fog of my dreams.

THREE

DIGNITY TAKES
A HOLIDAY

NOW I WAS HOME, AND it felt pretty damn good. A neighbor built a ramp up the back steps, and Ann-Marie fixed up a hospital room away from the hospital on the ground floor of the house. A cavalcade of teachers from Max's school showed up daily with the best homemade food imaginable. One night it was tortilla soup or homemade enchiladas, the next night fried chicken and pecan pie. But this went on for only a few days, and I felt an acute sense of loss when it stopped. The party was over. Now it was back to my mother-in-law's meat loaf and boiled potatoes.

I stayed in that modest ten-by-twelve-foot room for the next three years and got sick of it toward the end, but compared with the sterility of Cedars, it was the Ritz. I had every time-wasting electronic gadget I'd ever need and even a swimming pool outside to slide into whenever I felt so bold. The room got the best morning light of any room in the house and I could even peek out the window and see who was coming up the walk to visit me. If I didn't want to encounter a visitor, I would be "sleeping."

I felt a bit like a wild animal that had been captured, hospitalized, and rehabilitated and was now going through the gradual process of being reintroduced to its native surroundings. I knew I wasn't quite ready to bound back into the outback of human society. I was a little weak from six weeks in a hospital bed, but that really wasn't the problem. The problem was psychological. I was embarrassed, ashamed, and scared. I had been stripped of my dignity.

This problem of dignity is something that began during my hospital stay, but it didn't really hit me until I returned to the civilian world. Surrounded by stroke victims, you don't really measure yourself against normal, intact people. I was well aware of my physical infirmity, but this decline of self-worth sneaked up on me. Lost dignity is not something most of us think about before we lose it. We don't want people staring at our mismatched socks at our sister's wedding or some huffy Parisian waiter laughing at our pathetic attempt to order "boeuf" in high school French, but unless you're homeless, a stage three alcoholic, or Jimmy Swaggart caught with your pants down, most of us rarely experience full-blown shame. It's a terrifying state.

I doubt if I'm alone in fearing, deeply, the prospect of having my dignity snatched away in broad daylight. It probably dates back to the first grade and the bone-chilling prospect of looking down and seeing that somewhere between the drinking fountain and the fire drill, I'd had an "accident" and the next class was show-and-tell. Soon the principal would be announcing this mishap on the PA system. "Attention, all students, the Rucker boy has thoroughly soiled his britches and no one should point at him in class. Laugh all you want, but no pointing."

Martin Mull, coming of age in North Ridgeville, Ohio, actually had this experience and later reenacted the moment for an HBO special that was broadcast from his hometown. The piece was called "Stealing Home." Martin was about ten, playing in a hotly contested Little League baseball game on a late summer afternoon. He was on third base, the last chance for his team to tie the game in the last half of the last inning. The batter was a klutzy nonathlete named Lefty who was inexplicably batting right-handed, so things didn't look good. Martin's only shot at baseball immortality was to brazenly steal home.

Unfortunately, the excitement was too much for this young Lou Brock in training, and he peed all over himself, a yellow current trickling down his leg like the Ohio River during flood season. Smart boy that he was, Mull figured he'd steal home anyway, cover his embarrassment with the dirt of the slide, and be hoisted on the shoulders of his teammates for tying the game, his lapse of bladder control never revealed. He took off down the line; the pitcher saw him in plenty of time and tossed the ball home. Pee-boy was out by a mile. The game was over, his reputation as the go-to guy was in tatters, and when he stood up as the game's loser, the dirt and urine had turned into a conspicuous mud sculpture from his waist to his knees.

You get the point. We are all—from the heights of Court-ney Love to the depths of Jerry Springer's next guest—only one small faux pas away from deep humiliation. We seem to have a genetic imperative not to blubber in public, not to moon the audience on national television, not to shout "You really like me," not to get so drunk you take a leak in a pot-ted plant, not to sheepishly back down from a fistfight that you started, and a thousand other acts of dignity exposed and demolished.

That's why we laugh so hard at the same thing at the mov-ies. When we see John Candy mud-wrestling (and losing) in *Stripes*, we howl. When we see Ben Stiller get his thingy caught in his zipper in *There's Something About Mary*, we point and mock. But when it happens to us, we bury our heads in shame and try to steal home.

My late mother had a thing about keeping her dignity at all times, especially when she and her four children were out in public. There was no T-bone steak gnawing or toothpick picking at her table down at Murphy's Steak House. And if she thought she was being disrespected by a waiter because she was a single woman with four kids she could barely con-trol, she would, in a very dignified fashion, destroy the guy. He might wince at her acidic tongue-lashing about his use of the word "ain't," but the next time he brought coffee, it would be piping hot.

As much as the world irritated and frustrated her—which was often—I never saw my mother lose her dignity by shout-ing, cursing, spitting, cowering, wallowing, wailing, or belch-ing. Like the fictional heroine of the acclaimed TV-movie *The Autobiography of Miss Jane Pitman*, she always held her head high. Apparently this was not a trait I inherited from her, since I spent much of my life with my head in the "duck" position.

My current dignity problem began with the 911 encounter with Hans and Frans, the skeptical EMTs. It then continued with the infantile helplessness I experienced in the hospital, though not on any conscious level. At first, I kind of enjoyed the special status of the sick, at least the sick who can sit up in bed and chat with the un-sick. I was accorded an extra dollop of dignity for just popping jokes in such a predicament. Especially when I learned that there was a dim prospect of recovery, I tried to see myself as that skier with a broken leg. I had experienced a serious tumble, but soon I'd be back on the slopes regaling my friends with stories about the tree that had jumped in my way. I started to look forward to looking back on this horror, like the famous photo of President Lyndon Johnson, in his crude, country-boy fashion, raising his shirt and showing the world the foot-long surgical scar on his fat belly. A photo of my leaving the hospital in my wheelchair, my thumb high in the air, would make a great story for the grandkids.

But, back home, I came to realize that the hospital stay had rekindled some basic childhood fears and was but the first stage of an extended assault on my whole sense of self. I began to worry incessantly that some colossal bowel accident would happen again, this time in front of nonprofessionals. Having no clue as to what was going on "down there," I checked every fifteen minutes and headed for the bathroom every thirty. Thankfully, in my case, these major indignities didn't become chronic events. During this period, I read on the Internet that many severely impaired people—quadriplegics with additional complications, for instance—want to die not because they are in physical pain, but because every moment of their compromised, infantlike existence is bereft of human dignity. From just the few undignified accidents I'd already experienced, that made perfect sense to me.

Though seemingly free of the big, five-alarm indignities (though, of course, you never know), I soon became familiar with a thousand minor, often stupid, ones. Flipping over in my wheelchair, for instance. Early on, this would happen about twice a week. I would thrust forward, the chair would slip back, and there I'd be, on my back, feet in the air, flipped-turtle style. This rarely hurt and always looked more precarious to others than it really was, but I always felt foolish, and still do. Avoid magnanimous bear hugs from 200-pound friends when they drop by to cheer you up. You will probably end up under the computer table with your friend on top.

Searching on Google, I learned that paralytics have a high rate of drug and alcohol abuse. On the one hand, this makes sense, especially if you become paralyzed at a young age. It's a taxing, monumentally frustrating situation that invites self-medication. On the other hand, I began to wonder, how do all those wheel-based alcoholics and stoners stay upright? Once I had escaped from the alcohol-free zone of Cedars, I was ready for a glass of wine or two. Okay, three. Hey, I was paralyzed! A little brain-pickling seemed in order. Until I realized that I couldn't function in a chair under the influence. I'd turn sharply to reach for a wine bottle, lose my already precarious balance, and go down like a woozy middleweight.

To this day, feed me two and a half glasses of wine and I'm liable to end up in the turtle pose in front of the dinner guests. It's a hard situation to talk your way out of. "Darn that rug! Honey, we have got to tack that thing down." Intoxicants make you lose control when you're trying to do everything you can to maintain control. It's no fun to lose what you don't have much of to begin with.

I soon came to learn that, drunk or sober, you are always at a physical disadvantage, sometimes embarrassingly so. There is one startling moment of humiliation that still grates on me, a moment when I came to identify with every case of police abuse ever filed. About a week after I had come home from the hospital, Ann-Marie and I were alone one evening, working on adjusting to this new state. We had yet to do any retrofitting of the house to accommodate a wheelchair. I couldn't squeeze through the opening of the downstairs bathroom, so we had taken the door off and replaced it temporarily with a long curtain. Assuming I didn't lose my balance and fall off the makeshift attachment on top of our normal commode, I could pretty much take care of myself.

While I was, you might say, indisposed, there was a loud knock at the door. Ann-Marie answered it and faced a phalanx of LA's so-called finest. There was some hurried mumbling, and before anything was clear, two beefy patrolmen were stomping around the house like one of those drug raids you see on *Cops*. Someone in the neighborhood had apparently reported loud shouting going on in a nearby house and the cops had picked ours. They were looking for a wife beater or—as is often the case on *Cops*—a husband beater.

What they found, when they pulled back the curtain and glowered into the bathroom, billy clubs in hand, was me.

They stared for what seemed like an eternity, as if they had never seen a man in this pose before. They saw me as a potential criminal, not a crippled man on a toilet. It was as if they relished both their power and my indignity; I'm surprised they didn't take my wheelchair, just for fun. They left the curtain ajar, and without a word of apology to either Ann-Marie or me, walked out of the house. Their whole storm-trooper act was infuriating. It was a state-sanctioned home invasion. And I could do nothing, not even look at them eyeball to eyeball and tell them to get the hell out of my house. It was more than demeaning. It was castrating.

You can sit around a ten-by-twelve room for only so long, no matter how shaky and self-conscious you are, so I started taking short treks into the social habitat I had once known so well. I tried to keep the outings short and sweet—a Super Bowl party here, a cheap Italian restaurant there—but I still felt alien and out of place. Maybe the best way to describe it is that you feel like the only black guy at an all-white Kiwanis Club meeting. You've been invited to join the club and help out with the upcoming paper drive, but you're still a curiosity—a little intimidating, even scary, to some; awkward to be around for others. Everybody is walking on eggshells not to offend you. They all want you to know that *they* think you're perfectly normal. The black Kiwanian finds himself in a lot of overly friendly conversations about pro football, Mike Tyson, and "real" southern barbecue. The guy in the wheelchair finds himself in a lot of overly friendly conversations about Christopher Reeve, driving with hand controls, the unfairness of life, and hospital food.

The continuum of response, I soon learned, went from people who are kind to you to people who are way too kind. On my first trip to the supermarket, a nice old man approached me and handed me a lollipop, just to "put a smile on my face." He left without giving anyone else a lollipop, so I knew I was special.

My most abrupt encounter with the overly kind came a few months later. I had gotten a writing job with the meta-magicians Penn and Teller in Las Vegas; this was really stepping out into the untamed human jungle. I set out on a Sunday morning to grab a cup of coffee at the local Star-bucks. Las Vegas, at least physically, is the most user-friendly place on earth for handicapped people. Every hotel and hot spot, having been built in the last two weeks or so, is re-plete with ramps, handrails, elevators, escalators, you name it. Plus, Las Vegas caters to older Americans in wheelchairs who are bored with the grandkids and ready to blow their pension on a roll of the dice. There are special blackjack tables, slots, and other games designed especially for people in wheelchairs. They love crips in Vegas.

Anyway, I tooled up to this Starbucks on a bright Sunday morning, and there was a line out to the sidewalk. The night before, there had been a big concert by a now defunct music group, Phish—a laid-back, Grateful Dead–style dope-rock band with a dedicated following of young, chemically al-tered Phish-heads. One of those heads, no doubt stoned and awake since the Thursday before, stumbled up behind me, took one look at my chair, and went into action. He grabbed the chair handles, started pushing people out of the way, and maneuvered me right up to the front of the line. There, he announced to the world that he was buying me a cup of cof-fee for "everything this guy did for us in Nam, man. This guy, man, I mean, he took a bullet or something, you know...." His speech dribbled off incoherently, but everyone got the point. To him, I was a war hero. I fit the picture: I was in the right age group for Vietnam, was dressed like someone on a government pension, and had a wheelchair to back up my Purple Heart. I tried to tell him otherwise, but he wasn't listening. He was probably hallucinating his own rendition of the sappy Lee Greenwood anthem, "I'm Proud to Be an American."

I awkwardly extricated myself from this jam by convincing the guy that "Man, I don't take handouts, man, I always buy my own coffee, man, it's a thing with me, you with me, bro?" He could dig where I was coming from and left me alone. However misguided, this addled patriot gave me a good idea: go down to the Army-Navy store, pick out some camouflage gear, put a red-white-and-blue *schmata* on my head, and I'd never have to pay for a Starbucks again.

As I mostly shuffled around the house in those early weeks at home, venturing out and scurrying back on rare occasions, I wasn't making much emotional progress. All the ongoing bodily embarrassments, the acts of pity and condescension, and the occasional downright insult were getting to me, especially when I imagined this to be my permanent fate. As yet, I had no clear strategy to counter the humiliation and frustration I often felt, even when alone. You can't just tell yourself, "Hey, don't feel crappy!" when people treat you like a leper or rush to pick you up off the kitchen floor after you've done a half-gainer into a belly flop. It's like boot camp, I thought, though I never had the pleasure of boot camp myself. You just eat the humiliation and go on. Or you get kicked out of the army. Your choice.

The real surprise was not the discomfort and shame—I figured those were coming, though it was still a shock when they hit and kept on hitting. In my cluelessness, I began to sense something else. I began to think there might be an odd therapeutic effect to all this ignominy. There could be a good side to losing control that I had never counted on. My logic, however twisted, went like this:

I was clearly, at age fifty-one, strung out from years of stress, worry, and self-doubt. No matter what I did, especially in the ten years leading up to this event, I had seemed helpless to find the right professional or financial track. I kept throwing balloons into the air, and they kept popping. I once told a shrink that my work-related goal in life was simple: to find something that I could do "repetitively and well." I was no closer to that goal in December 1996 than I had been in December 1986 or December 1976. And the clock was running.

Of course I wasn't really helpless to direct my life down a sensible path. I had just taken a lot of missteps, many of them spurred on by an inflated sense of my own worth or talent, at least in the cut-and-dried marketplace of Hollywood. I stuck it out because I had already invested twenty-some years looking for a profitable niche in show business; it wasn't as though I had come out here for a summer internship and decided that this was not my cup of tea. Pride, in other words, had a lot to do with my situation. Of course I couldn't see that at the time. All I saw was the next gig around the corner, the one that was going to finally be the big score that changed everything. As someone once said, you can die of encouragement in Hollywood. I was dying of no one's encouragement but my own. My sense of helplessness was entirely self-induced.

A very talented documentary maker, Tom Cohen, made a film in 1982 as part of a limited PBS series, "Middletown," about life in Muncie, Indiana, a town that had been the focus of an earlier groundbreaking sociological study by Robert Lynd. The film was called *Family Business*, and it was about a man who owned and operated a Shakey's Pizza franchise in Muncie. He loved the business—he did all the local radio ads himself and even got on a little stage at the restaurant and performed for the customers—but he wasn't a good franchise owner. He was going broke fast. He employed his wife and all nine kids trying to keep the pizza place afloat, but it wasn't happening.

The scene that will forever stick with me takes place when the family gathers around the dinner table toward the end of the film to discuss what to do. In essence, everyone in the room knows what to do—throw in the towel—except the man himself. He can't see it—he's too attached to his dream. Watching him grapple with this bitter truth was like watching Willy Loman getting fired from his salesman job.

Maybe the best thing that could have happened to that fellow was to end up in a hospital bed for a few weeks, genuinely helpless and dependent on others. One bout with overt, concrete helplessness might have helped him transcend the psychological helplessness and defeat he felt about his business. It's like hitting rock bottom. Everything you do after that is up. Confronting and coping with the fundamental problems of sitting, walking, and using the toilet can carry over, on some level of will and intent, to confronting and coping with other problems you feel you can't control. Mastering a wheelchair, in other words, might just feed the belief that you can master your life.

Now, there was a thought that could get me up in the morning and moving from the bed to the computer all of four feet away, having checked three or four times for accidents. The hypothesis had yet to be tested, of course, and it just added another wrinkle to my then thoroughly confused outlook. The question kept coming up in my head: how *am* I supposed to feel about becoming a cripple? I pondered the four classic choices, according to an old shrink: mad, glad, sad, or scared. I certainly felt no compulsion to feel glad, but I didn't seem that mad, either. That confused me. Why, for instance, wasn't I furious, enraged, apoplectic with anger and bile, throwing chairs against the wall, cursing God, starting fights in crowded elevators? Sure, I yelled "This isn't fair!" and "Fuck you, universe!" at the top of my lungs a few times in the middle of the night, but that was short-term venting, not long-term rage. I was frustrated, but never a threat to myself or others. Why not?

I concluded that it had something to do with my age and perhaps the scar tissue that had resulted from a lifetime of sporadic angry outbursts. My response, I decided, was "age-appropriate." I was a middle-aged fellow, with an intact family and a long if spotty résumé. In the pursuit of a respectable life, I already had a leg up. In fact, I could have probably bailed out, more or less, and still had a few accomplishments to look back on. I didn't *have* to wheel back into the world and craft a career, build a family, or otherwise prove my worth, on top of worrying about having a bladder accident or feeling like a freak. I was close enough to the ninth inning to call the game and quietly retire to the farm.

At an earlier age, I probably would have been much more outwardly bitter and pissed. It's one thing to be cheated out of your legs, another to be cheated out of your legs, your youth, and your virility. At twenty-five, I would have told the drugged-out Starbucks guy in Vegas to fuck off and leave me alone, Jack, I can get my own coffee. I would have carried a permanent chip on my shoulder and been itching to confront anyone who ignored, insulted, or patronized me.

In my early encounters with the outside world, I did feel the urge to yell at rude and inconsiderate people or complain up the chain of command when I couldn't get into the store. But I usually held back. The huffing and puffing were trumped by something I felt was more critical—the fact that I didn't want to define myself as a disabled person, still less as an unpleasant disabled person. These labels are useful only when you're trying to get something important done, like the man in Alabama who couldn't get up the courthouse steps and had to go to the Supreme Court to get an elevator. That's the time to wave the disability flag proudly. But most of the time the issue is not a grave civil injustice; lives are not at stake, nor even your perceived worth as a human being. It can be a hassle, and the experience of looking into the eyes of some workaday store employee who couldn't care less can be infuriating. But unless you're one of those types who like to file a class-action suit every time a bathroom sink is not the right height, you'd best let it pass and move on to the next store.

I decided to pick my fusses carefully to avoid being typecast as a "disabled guy." From the moment I left the hospital and reentered the natural world, I kept waffling between "Don't treat me any differently" and "Of course, treat me differently; be kinder, more thoughtful; I'm special." Finally, "Don't treat me any differently" came to have far greater value. The truth is that, like probably every other wheelchair user, I do not want to be defined in any way by this freakish turn of fate and the shape it has left me in. It's the same, I'm sure, with a black actor who would rather be thought of as an "actor" or a female executive who would prefer to be just an "executive." It's fine with me if the paralysis is a source of curiosity and even humor, but it shouldn't confer on me any special status, good or bad. It's just what it is.

This is a point worth repeating: one of the biggest hurdles you have to overcome after becoming paralyzed is not to have others define you—and not to define *yourself*—by this one obvious thing. A healthy view of yourself demands that paralysis not be the center of your existence. Early on you are so overwhelmed by it that it does define you, or at least it dominates your thinking and your daily presentation of self.

Only a couple of weeks after I had gone home, one of Max's eight-year-old friends came for dinner one evening. About halfway through the meal, having listened to me blather on about every nuance of my paraplegic day, he blurted out, "Why don't you stop talking about your paralysis thing all the time and talk about something fun?"

"Duly noted," I felt like saying, "now get the hell out of my house." As much as he bothered me, the kid had a point. I was doing the very thing I was striving not to do—letting the paralysis dominate my every thought. I'm sure Max was ready to change the subject too.

Again, age seems a big factor in all this. At my age, it was much easier to present my condition as something that happened *to* me as opposed to something I *am*. Old friends don't see the paralysis at all—they just see the same old jerk, now in a permanent sitting position. Early on, my brother Ralph gave me what I consider a high compliment by saying that I was "the least handicapped handicapped person he had ever met." Of course he has known me every year of my life. There was no way he would see the chair first and the person in the chair second.

But most people, at least in public, do see the chair first. It's hard to miss. So in a new situation, you yourself often think of the chair first, too, and want to talk about it. This is seldom a good idea. I remember the first class I taught at the USC School of Cinema-TV after becoming paralyzed. I was very nervous. I was well prepared to talk about the subject of the class—television documentaries—but was very unsure about how to handle the subject of the wheelchair. I was still at a tender point where I and the paralysis were just one confusing entity, so I went with the up-front approach. "As you've no doubt noticed," I said at the outset, "I'm in a wheelchair, and I know you're saying to yourself, 'Why is this guy in a wheelchair?' So let me tell you, so at least I won't be nervous about being here in this wheelchair, which I am. . . ."

In retrospect, it was a stupid thing to do, and I never did it again. I could tell from their faces that neither my "tragedy" nor the wheelchair was on their minds. They were much more focused on what they were going to have to do in this course this semester to get a decent grade. "Are there any papers to write?" they wondered. "Do I have to talk in class? How much will the final exam count toward my grade?" I felt embarrassed for even bringing the paralysis up. They didn't give a hoot.

Once you've experienced the whole glorious assortment of pride-bruising indignities that paralysis can often bring about—the wet spot on your pants leg, the offensive odor that hits everyone in a crowded elevator, doing the turtle flip at the wedding reception, getting stuck in an aisle at Nordstrom's, having to be hauled up a long flight of stairs like a beanbag chair, or (worst of all) being either gawked at or invisible in public—you go through all that crap, and then one day you suddenly get it.

It hits you like the evangelist Oral Roberts whopping you in the face with the fiery right hand of God—*No one gives a damn! It doesn't matter! No one really cares!* Most people, in most situations, are like those college kids—they have something much more important on their minds, something central to their own lives. Most of the time, the people you think are dissing you are just trying to get by you and get on with their own game plans. They are rarely if ever focused on you, no matter how freakish or undignified you feel. They are focused on *themselves*. They are thinking, Why is this guy bothering *me*?—not How can I accommodate this disabled soul? In the best of scenarios, such encounters with the ambulatory world are win-win. You bring someone, at least momentarily, out of their fog of self-obsession; you get accommodated; and they feel good about themselves. By asking them to carry you up some stairs like a beanbag chair, you are actually doing them a favor.

We all want to be treated like the Exceptional One— the funniest, the smartest, the best dressed, the sexiest, the weirdest. But when you become the involuntary exception, it messes with your sense of self—and your sense of dignity—in a whole new way. Indignities abound, but at least you know pretty much how the world sees you—your identity is now grounded in this obvious thing—so you can belie expectations by not taking yourself, or "it," too seriously. It won't end discrimination, racial or disabled, and it ain't a cure for paralysis; but the black guy at the Kiwanis meeting could do worse than put his arm around his chubby host with the sheepish smile and tell his favorite Mike Tyson joke. Hell, everybody likes a good Mike Tyson joke.

FOUR

CRIPPLE DOS
AND DON'TS

WE ALL HAVE OUR OWN cornball ways of dealing with anything, including becoming paralyzed, and I was slowly figuring
out my approach. I like to make up rules. Growing up in the
1950s, I was a big, big fan of the educational and industrial
films we were force-fed in elementary and junior high school (a
company called Coronet made a lot of them). Martin Mull once
summed up the whole experience with one title: "Aluminum,
Our Shiny Friend." I gravitated toward the more personal filmic
guides to social behavior, especially those involving dating and
petting (most of them), hygiene, grooming, and how to spot a
communist. God knows you wouldn't want to be trying to get
to "first base" with the daughter of a dirty godless commie.

Having outgrown the caring paralytic nursery of Cedars-Sinai and now venturing ever farther from my home base into the world at large, I felt as if I were back in Mrs. Wright's fifth-grade class, trying to learn the intricacies of how to present myself. I had all the emotional maturity of a fifth-grader—I was shy, scared, and deathly afraid of doing or saying something colossally stupid. I needed to know the basics, the adult equivalent of how to make small talk with the mother of a girl I had a crush on. "Good afternoon, Mrs. Anderson, that is an awfully pretty dress you're wearing," I came to find out, would get you a lot farther than "Hi, toots, where's that trashy daughter of yours?" As unschooled as a ten-year-old Romeo, I really didn't know how to be a paralytic, how to behave in public so that people wouldn't treat me like their grandfather or walk away mumbling, "Jeez, what a bitter, angry, sad person he is!" You don't want the coddling, you don't want the confrontation. You just want to make a good impression, as you did with Veronica's mom, assuming your hair was combed, your shirttail was tucked in, and you didn't refer to the size of her breasts.

There were also educational films on how to deal with a school bully, who was, after all, just a lonely kid looking for attention. In the fifth grade of paralysis, hateful bullies are a rarity, at least where I live. Friendly bullies, the overly kind types mentioned earlier, were the ones freaking me out. Along with the people who just flat-out ignore you, these were the segment of society toward whom I had to learn the proper, Coronet-style behavior.

Take the common experience of not being seen, for instance, because you are forever fifty-four inches tall or, if you slump, fifty-two inches. There is a right way and a wrong way of dealing with, say, a self-absorbed, aisle-blocking chatterbox at a crowded party. The wrong way would be to say, with a certain snap in your voice, "Could you get the hell out of my way, please?" That would only peg you as the belligerent disabled guy who no one will ever invite back to their party. The right way is a nonthreatening tap on the shoulder while you say, "Excuse me, sir," and keeping to yourself the thought, What an insufferable prick. The person will smile the kind of smile he reserves for old ladies and homeless guys with tin cups and politely step aside. You then give a little thank-you wave and go on your way.

See? It's simple when you know the rules.

Let's face it: proper wheelchair etiquette demands fresh thinking in the area of social problem solving and in some cases crisis management. And often you don't see the problem until it is right in your face. At the same party where the blowhard blocks your path, for instance, your host will worry that people will trip over you, as they will, repeatedly, forcing the host to work hard to find just the right spot for you to park so that "you can see everybody." That spot will probably be in the corner, far away from the foot traffic and the fully stocked bar..."the best seat in the house." The host will then leave to mingle. Everyone is mingling. Parties = mingling. Mingling in a wheelchair is impossible in most homes and apartments. Remember the famous elbow-to-elbow party scene in *Breakfast at Tiffany's*? A person in a wheelchair in that madhouse would have been crushed like an errant bonbon.

So you're parked, you're drinking, you're smiling and waving, hoping someone you know will wander over to chat. But they rarely do, even your closest friends. First, you're hard to see behind the potted plant and the twelve guests standing in front of it; and, second, they're all mingling! Mingling means maintaining standing eye contact with the other standing guests when you're not moving from room to room, looking to make more eye contact with more standing guests. The seated guest in the corner is completely out of everyone's line of sight. You're like the little kid tugging on his papa's jacket, saying, "Hey, talk to me, talk to me!"

You have no choice but to wait, nursing that watery Scotch right down to the last chip of ice. There's not a chance in hell of getting to the bar for another. Finally, someone sits down who knows no one at the party, including you. This person invariably loves to talk about chronic illness, the Canadian health care system, the restorative power of prayer, or all three. He or she figures that you, in your impaired condition, know about all these topics and will love to trade "war stories." Soon you're either diagnosing your new friend's mother's pesky diverticulitis or fending off signing up for their Prayer-a-Day phone service. There is no way that you can gracefully slide away on spotting "my very oldest friend" coming in the door. Graceful exits and wheelchairs don't mix. You're stuck, dude. Either you join in the discussion of the diseases of man or you feign narcolepsy and nod off, which is extremely rude and rarely convincing. What to do?

A wheelchair counterpart of Miss Manners would offer you three choices. One, ask the person to get you another drink, and while he or she is gone, locate the host and repark in another room. Two, introduce this medical magpie to someone who appears to have just been sick or to be getting sick and hope they'll hit it off and wander off together in search of vitamin C. Three, announce that you're leaving the party. You immediately head for the door, scraping shins and damaging toes along the way, and if no one stops to talk to you before you get to the exit, you're forced to go home, hours early and with hardly a buzz. Since you've yet to learn to drive on your own with hand controls, you have to drag your spouse along as your chauffeur, and she was having the best time she's had since you became paralyzed. You then have to fake a severe gastric problem to trump her disappointment.

You go to bed, depressed, promising yourself that in the future you will limit your social outings to grocery shopping or small sit-down dinner parties with non-hypochondriacs.

The solution to every problem like this is to anticipate. A savvy partygoer in a wheelchair would have sent a scout out a day or two in advance to check out the location of the house, the location of the bar, and the most advantageous place to park for maximum exposure, probably right next to the front door or the hallway leading to the bathroom. "Oh, you really have to go? I'll see you when you come out...." If you can't send a scout and are a complete wing nut about mingling, have your host send along location photos.

Here's another common scenario in which anticipation is crucial. You're on your way to an important business meeting and you've concentrated so hard on your winning sales pitch that you've forgotten to inquire about the meeting site. You show up and find yourself facing three flights of stairs and no elevator because the guy you're meeting decided it would be hip to have an office in an old fire station. If there's no alternative, someone will have to haul you up the stairs. Make sure your business host has at least three hefty male associates with no back problems so there are no bad feelings or lawsuits. You don't want to be manhandled like this, of course, but it's far less embarrassing than trying to conduct the meeting in an underground parking garage.

In conducting business, I discovered during this Coronet phase, conference phone calls are perfect for wheelchair users. People will still laugh at your jokes, assuming they're funny, and you'll never catch someone gawking at your lower body, mouth half-open, wondering, Jeez, how does he live like that?

In terms of more casual social affairs, old friends know what to expect and are ready with a portable ramp for the front steps or the most convenient table setting. New friends, on the other hand, are often caught off guard unless you are courteous enough to walk through the evening with them by phone or E-mail beforehand. Make a checklist—begin with level parking and whether or not their only downstairs facility is a converted broom closet with a nine-inch-wide doorway. Save the touchy subjects until last, like their frisky 120-pound Rottweiler who loves kids but thinks wheelchairs are an alien breed invading his territory. It's no fun dodging a dog's viselike grip on your left foot every time you move, even if you can't feel the pain.

With bigger outings, like an intercontinental flight or a family vacation, planning ahead is not only socially correct; it is imperative. Think about it. You're on a ten-hour nonstop flight from LA to London. After the considerable hassle of going from your wheelchair to a narrower "aisle" chair and being shoehorned into your seat, you kick back like anyone else and buckle up. They bring you your food, your entertainment, your blanket, and your ice cream sundae. But, alas, they don't bring you the bathroom.

There is no way that a paralyzed passenger can leave his

or her seat on an airplane and stroll down to the loo. First of all, your wheelchair is in the baggage hold. Second, even if you could get to the toilet, you couldn't get through the door, let alone swing around to transfer. A proper-sized washroom for handicapped passengers on a commercial airplane would take up half of first class. Your choices are limited. You can take the Mahatma Gandhi approach—don't eat or drink anything for three days before the flight and chew only on the pillow during it. Or you can bow to all the temptations the flight attendant can serve you, including endless refills of your Diet Coke, by arranging to wear a permanent catheter and an unexposed bag for such a long haul. This solution is actually quite simple and worry-free. The apparatus is totally undetectable, and no one will give it, or you, a second thought, unless an inquisitive type looks across the aisle and asks, "How in the world is that poor sap supposed to relieve himself at thirty-thousand feet?" (If asked, say you practice a brand of yoga that allows you to suspend bladder function for three or more time zones; then go into a meditative trance.)

Of course, you can plan ahead all you want, and disaster may still come knocking. Even the most thoughtful wheelchair user is prone to overlook the smallest of details, like the wobbly little wheel on the front of the chair that can turn a civilized dinner party into a forty-five-minute search for a very small Allen wrench. And the more details there are to anticipate, the more things will go wrong. It goes with the territory.

I stuck the word "anticipate" at the top of my computer screen, but the message took years to sink in. The very first vacation we took after I became paralyzed—over five and a half years later—was an early-in-the-season trip to the incomparable Martha's Vineyard off the coast of Massachusetts. It sounded like the right thing to do. "Oh, yes, we just got back from the Vineyard; the weather was to die for, but the traffic!..." Through a travel agent friend, we made all the right arrangements and checked them twice. We arrived in Boston to find a rental car with hand controls waiting for us. We had reserved a place on the ferry to the island six months in advance. In a vacation spot where every hotel room is precious, we had booked the quaintest little "whaling ship captain's home" of a hotel near the water that had reserved their only handicapped-accessible "carriage house" cottage for our pleasure. A dream vacation was in the offing.

Until we got to the carriage house. Apparently "accessible" means something different to Yankees, and it certainly meant something different to the people who had built this cottage with wooden nails in 1704. For one thing, they didn't like to waste a lot of space on doorways—probably out of some Puritan aversion to obesity. Suffice it to say that I scraped my knuckles squeezing through the front door, and there was no way in hell that my chair could wiggle through the two little wall slits from bed to bath. This place was worse than inaccessible; I couldn't move without knocking over some prerevolutionary bric-a-brac. Also, someone had decided to replace the main sewer pipe three feet from our front door the night we arrived. It was handicapped hell, paid for in advance.

The innkeeper shrugged—some underling had apparently dropped the ball—and we were up the creek. Ann-Marie and Max left me curled up on the bed as they took a stroll along the water. As fate would have it, they spotted a big Victorian-era hotel with a big ramp in front, and our prayers were answered. The place happened to have one handicap-accessible room vacant, complete with a Sunday night discount. With one swipe of a credit card, we went from a 1704 stockade to a fin de siècle palace with handrails. The hotel is called the Harbor View, and it has a gargantuan porch for sitting, smoking a stogie, and staring across the ocean toward France. Check it out the next time you're in the area.

Put this in your disability rule book and underline it twice. No matter what the social engagement on your calendar, big or small, you could miss out on a lot of fun if you are too nice, too gracious, and too fearful of offending and don't ask a lot of irritating questions like "What is the width of the bathroom door to the half inch?" or "Do you have a muzzle or maybe some Xanax for that Rottweiler?"

Paralytics like me have to learn the rules of proper disabled behavior, but the good-hearted ambulatory citizen, or 99 percent of everyone else out there, must also know how to deal with the ambulatory-challenged in any social situation. And even before your first encounter, you must tackle the thorny issue of what to call us. "Ambulatory-challenged," for instance, gets the point across politely but may have some slow learners running to the dictionary. The same is true with an even more upbeat label, "non-ambulatory-gifted," though everybody likes to be called gifted, if only out of pity.

Let's draw some uncrossable lines. "Gimp" or "crip" is totally unacceptable out of the mouth of the Average Walking Joe or Jane. It can be used only by paralytics referring to themselves, in the same way that only Richard Pryor or Chris Rock can make jokes using the N word and only a fat actress can refer to herself as a fat actress. It's insider talk, as in, "Hey, gimp, what's happening?" "Not much, gimp, I just won the LA Marathon, Wheelchair Division." "Wow, you are some mofo gimp!"

Initially, I was happy with the moniker "handicapped." It seems to have worked for centuries; but as part of the general ethnic, racial, and functional relabeling going on in America, it apparently has lost its magic. "Differently-abled" and "mobility-challenged" seem to be the most acceptable alternatives, especially if you live in Oregon and paint directional signs for public ramps. "Alternatively-abled" also has its fans, but it scared me a little. It seems to imply that a wheelchair user like me is able, or should be able, to do extraordinary things that normal people can't do, like spin a wheelie across a dance floor, bounce up a long flight of stairs with the deftness of a paralytic Fred Astaire, or play golf from a sitting position. Some people do all those things, of course, but they are as alternatively-abled as the alternatively-abled. You'd have to identify them as the "alternatively-alternatively-abled." Try getting that on a placard for your car.

Before you graduate from the grade school of paralysis, you have to learn that there are a slew of disability-related words in common, everyday usage that drive the disabled up the wall. Even after eight years in a chair, I still use many of them unconsciously and feel stupid when this is pointed out to me by a fellow wheelchair user. Of course, some distasteful terms I go out of my way to use simply because they are disarming. "Crippled," for instance—hence the title of this chapter. It is such a ridiculous, old-fashioned, pre-ADA word that it's fun to break the ice around the ambs by using it in reference to myself and my "type." It's like southerners calling themselves crackers or hillbillies. Don't you call them that, you arrogant easterner, but they can refer to themselves with a slur like this because their own families, friends, or hometowns are involved.

Now you're about to learn something, so grab a number 2 pencil and some paper. Refrain from using the whole lexicon of terms that make a disability sound like a death sentence. "Afflicted," for instance. As in, "He is afflicted with transverse myelitis, poor dear." No, I acquired it, as it were, and now it is just something I have. You wouldn't say, "He is afflicted with a beer belly or bushy eyebrows," would you? It's not a curse of the gods or the pockmark of eternal damnation. It's just a physical change.

Also, in describing a disabled person, avoid all words that make others cringe and feel pity and make someone like me feel I should be much worse off than I actually am. Thanks to the California Governor's Committee on Employment of People with Disabilities, here is a partial list of these offending terms:

- suffers from
- victim
- stricken
- confined
- struggling with
- unfortunate
- deformed
- defective
- poor
- spastic or spazzy
- lame
- maimed

I know—to some of you freethinkers, such linguistic rule-making is silly, stiff, and damn near un-American; but there is something substantive at work here. All these woe-is-me words are labels, connoting endless pain and suffering, a way of branding people as miserable and pathetic. "To label is to libel," as Marshall McLuhan was fond of saying. A few of you are now muttering, "Oh, get off it, a crip is a crip, and if that poor, stricken, unfortunate, deformed, struggling, defective, spazzy wheelchair-confined guy isn't a victim, who is?" Think of it like someone caught in a tornado in Junction City, Arkansas. That person was a "victim" of that tornado and "suffered from" getting his double-wide blown away, but ten years later you wouldn't continue to call him a victim. That would be stupid. It's something that happened, and life goes on. Just as with paralysis.

Or, hell, continue to use those off-putting words if you feel strongly that someone in a wheelchair or otherwise disabled has been irreversibly damaged and condemned to a life of misery and shame. But if you're going to call me a victim, please send a weekly check. We poor, afflicted victims need your money to feel better about ourselves.

As I was learning these linguistic guidelines, I concluded that we should deep-six all of them and agree on one label that both sets the disabled apart and makes us as equal as the next guy. Since the next guy has probably got a hyphen—Swedish-American, for instance, like my wife; or Raider-American, like an Oakland football fan—the disabled community should have a hyphen, too: Handicapped-American. Then we could have Handicapped-American holidays (every Monday is fine with me), Handicapped-American History Month ("Who invented the modern wheelchair?"), and a Handicapped-

American caucus in the House of Representatives (but only for the physically, not the morally, impaired). Just a thought. No letters, please. I'm not buying "Differently-Abled-Americans," although DAA has a nice ring to it.

Labeling, of course, can work both ways. Dr. Rovner told me that when he worked in a rehab hospital in Chicago, the patients had a name for the staff who got them back into fighting shape after their car accidents or strokes: "temporarily ambulatory people," or TAP. The message was this: you're not in a wheelchair now, but you will be soon, so let up a little on the sit-ups, the early morning swim class, and all that jive about my "affliction."

Now that we know what to call the disabled and how not to describe their condition, it's time to move on to the right way to behave around them. This is not hard. Try to look them in the eye, not in the legs. Try not to gasp or turn away in horror, mumbling, "There but for the grace of God go I." When you are blocking their way in a restaurant, try to get out of the way calmly and not mutter, "I'm sorry; I'm so sorry; I'm so very, very sorry," as if you've just stepped on the neck of someone's kitten. With these and a few more commonsense tips in mind, you're halfway to being a handicapped-lover, or maybe a non-ambulatory-gifted-lover, if only in the nonbiblical meaning of the word.

For example, when encountering a person in a wheelchair:

- Don't shout in their ears. They're not deaf; they just can't walk. This is an important distinction.
- If you must shout, please never shout, "How's the

weather down there?" It's hard to respond with the downpour of spittle coming from your mouth.

- Never say to a wheelchair user as he or she pulls into parking spots reserved for the handicapped, "Man, you're lucky! I had to park seven spots away and walk!" They won't feel sorry for you.

- While in public, don't jerk Junior's arm off when he stares at a person in a wheelchair, nor say to him, "See, that will happen to you if you don't start minding me, young man!"

- Don't try to pass along your homily-filled philosophy about "living for today" and "God gives us only what we can handle" in the space of an elevator ride. "What floor, please?" will suffice.

- On that same elevator ride, don't ask, "So, bud, how did it happen?" just as the door opens and the person in the chair is late for a dental appointment. You're liable to hear, "The gun I'm carrying went off by mistake."

- Watch your toes at all times. Open-toe shoes are not recommended around wheelchairs. Construction boots, if they fit your outfit, are a much better choice.

- Finally, never, ever pat a person in a wheelchair on the head and say, "You are doing a super job of dealing with this!" You might end up getting your very own parking placard.

These are all valuable pointers, but only a starter kit for those who wish to lighten the load for people in wheelchairs. For instance, the injunction against shouting "How's the weather down there?" could be expanded to include, "Slow down or I'll have to give you a speeding ticket," "Can I hitch a ride?" and "You need a beeper on that thing—you could hurt somebody!" These are just a few of the ways that people feel compelled to announce in public, "You're in a wheelchair and I know it!" It's like they're reminding you in case you've forgotten.

As much as people try to avoid you, or accost you, in public, and as much as you try to go about your business without undue hassles, there are inevitable confrontations that demand you do something besides nod like a cluck and keep wheeling. Many of those confrontations involve parking. No one seems to resent the extra-wide toilet stalls with handrails for the handicapped—the non-impaired tend to use them with impunity—and you don't hear a lot of grumbling about the special handicapped section in the last row at the movie theater, since no one wants to sit back there anyway. But the convenience of handicapped parking strikes many as rank favoritism, which of course it is. That little parking placard (blue in California) just reeks of "I'm special and you're not." Ironically, what was created as a badge of immobility has become a badge of privilege, not a good thing in mythically classless America.

"Yeah, right" is the blunt response of many hurried drivers. There are many ways this can get expressed. One is to blithely park the minivan in the handicapped space right in front of the Super Store, knowing that your chances of getting caught are probably no worse than your chances of getting caught with your dog off the leash. This is expensive risk-taking. In the city of Los Angeles, for instance, the parking patrol writes about 30,000 citations a year for violations of handicapped parking spaces. And the fine can be pricey, from $330 in LA to much more elsewhere. In the city of Glendale, adjacent to LA, the fine is $1,200. Did you save that much time?

It's best for scofflaws to display some kind of placard, even an out-of-date one. The cops don't look that closely. You could steal one from an unlocked car, or better yet, buy a fake one from the underground placard trade. According to one source, there are approximately 400,000 valid placards in use in Los Angeles and twice as many fake ones in circulation. The word on the street is that you can buy them at flea markets or anyplace where fake Rolex watches and Chinese-made Gucci handbags are sold. The going rate in LA is about $25 a pop. (Prices may vary in your area.) At that rate, you can give the placards out as presents at the office Christmas party.

Don't tell me this is a petty public concern. When you can market 800,000 fake anything in a city like this, that's a lucrative racket. Someone out there is getting rich off the crippled people.

Not that it's very hard to get an official placard from the DMV and save your $25. Generally, all it takes is a letter from your doctor, the same doctor who gave you a prescription for Valium because "life" was making you nervous. Play your cards right and you can get a placard because you have a trick knee. I began to take close note of who had these placards, and my early research indicated that an inordinate number of people with no visible disability or impairment displayed one proudly. Maybe the sign really belonged to an invalid at home—though this would still be a clear parking violation—or maybe the driver had a heart condition or some other perfectly legitimate albeit invisible health problem (such as lung disease, low vision, or diabetes) that necessitated the convenience. Far be it from me to cast aspersions because someone who seems a little too healthy has just taken the only available handicapped spot in three square miles and was last seen running at full speed into the department store white sale. This person very well might be willing to die of late-stage emphysema just to get the last duvet at 50 percent off. You never can tell.

Occasionally someone crosses the line in the handicapped parking wars and you have to defend your territory. It can get ugly out there. I read about a disabled man in Florida who was arrested after brandishing a sword during a flap with another disabled man over a parking space. He must have just seen *Braveheart*. The strangest incident of this kind in my experience occurred after I had learned to drive with hand controls and just after I had gotten out of the hospital following one of my many weeklong infection-related trips. I was feeling perky and wanted to buy a book, so I drove down to the local mall. All the handicapped spots were filled—remember, there are 1.2 million real and fake placards in LA and probably 314 actual spots. In one space, I noticed, was a big, blowsy lady in a fuchsia-colored hot pants ensemble circa 1976 who seemed to be moving shoe boxes from the backseat of her Toyota to the trunk in anticipation of leaving. So I pulled up and politely asked, "Are you about to leave?"

She turned in a huff and stared me down. "Do I look like I'm about to leave? 'Cause I'm here to tell you, I ain't leaving. You can write down my license plate if you want, but I ain't leaving." She then got back into her car and turned the radio up to kick-out-the-jams level, no doubt to drown out the incessant .

chirping of insects like me. I got the clear message that I wasn't the first crabby placard waver to inquire about that space.

I toured the lot, looking for another space and plotting my next move. I pulled up beside her again and politely pointed out that she was in a disabled spot and had no placard. "See, I'm paralyzed, you see," I said, "and need to be close to that elevator, because, ah, that's the way things are set up. Are you yourself disabled?" (I was clearly goading her at this point.)

She again turned like a charging bull, raising her arms high and wide. "Do I look like I'm disabled?" she shouted, doing a 360-degree turn like a whacked-out runway model. She said it three times, as if I were hard of hearing (see guideline 1 above). "Then you're breaking the law," I said. At this point she glared at me like I was a dead man, gave me the finger, turned the radio up even louder, and went back to shuffling shoe boxes from seat to trunk.

Luckily, another car pulled out of a disabled spot nearby and I pulled in. I figured this was the end of my encounter with the brazen trespasser nee hit woman. Still, I was so freaked out by her volatility that I tried to wheel up to the elevator as inconspicuously as possible, head lowered almost to waist level, to avoid further contact. It didn't work. As I rolled past, I heard one last verbal uppercut.

"Hey, wheelchair boy, I hope you're paralyzed because someone kicked the shit out of you!"

That did it. That pissed me off. Steal my parking place, fine. Give me the finger and think I'm deaf, fine. But don't rejoice in my condition. I rolled upstairs and had the store people call security to check on this woman. I was worried about the next person in a chair—she might decide to kick the shit out of him.

An hour later I returned to my car, figuring that the woman was either gone or waiting in the shadows with a tire iron. When the elevator door opened, the scene was like an episode of *Cops*. Two LAPD cars had blocked her car, still in the same spot, and the officers had Ms. Hot Pants in handcuffs against the wall. Four or five security guys were standing around, rubbernecking. I felt a little guilty, so I asked one of them, "Did I do a good thing or bad thing by calling you in?" "Oh, a good thing," he said. "That crazy woman wouldn't budge and now she and her car are going downtown. I sure wasn't going to mess with her. Hell, I'm just security."

When I was safely away, I realized that I wasn't really mad at this woman. In a way, I admired her take-no-prisoners attitude. She could have been cranked on speed or just nuts, but I'm sure she thought she had a right to that space and screw all the whiny placard elitists who tried to shame her out of it, the special people demanding special treatment. Her life was no doubt pretty crappy too. Why shouldn't she get a break now and then?

It didn't take me long in my education as a disabled person to see that the pendulum of unfair advantage swings both ways. There are a myriad of ways that wheelchair users, at least the cagey ones, angle to exploit their condition and get the rest of the world to do their bidding. There are tricks, in other words, to the disability trade, and it's only fair to point some of them out. I guess this Coronet film would be called "You May Be Disabled, but Hey, You're Not Helpless!" The lead character would be Bobby, a twelve-year-old kid in a wheelchair who takes you through his average day and shows you all the devious tricks that he can pull to get his way.

The alarm goes off—it's another school day. If Bobby is sufficiently paralyzed but not someone who genuinely needs functional assistance, he can still get Mom or Sis to bring him his clothes, the morning sports section, and his laptop, and perhaps even dress him. "Gosh, I'm sorry, Mom, I forgot to lay out my shirt, pants, shoes, socks, and iPod next to my bed. Could you get them for me?" This personal assistant could be called the Handi-Valet.

It goes on from there. Bobby knows how to punch all the right buttons. "Gee, could you fix me breakfast, Mom? I can't reach the Post Toasties." "Could you drive me to school? The bus is such a pain." "Could you wheel me up the ramp at school? My arms are tired from eating Post Toasties." "Mrs. Johnson, I have to go to the washroom—I'll be back in an hour and a half." If it's raining or below thirty-two degrees Fahrenheit, Bob-o doesn't have to go to school at all. Inclement weather is an excellent excuse for any person in a wheelchair to stay home, and almost everyone buys it without question.

In school, our crafty little friend can buy himself an easy A in English by writing a heartfelt essay entitled "What It's Like to Be Me." In history, the A essay is "The Americans with Disabilities Act and the Supreme Court." In biology, it's "What Is a Stem Cell and Why Do We Care?" Also, all the kids in the hallway will wave to Bobby whether they like him or not. Most likely, the biggest, meanest middle line-backer on the football team will think of Bobby as his own personal "Rudy" and call him "my special pal."

After school, Bobby can easily talk his mother into allow-ing him to play "Grand Theft Auto—San Andreas" for three hours because he can't go X-treme skateboarding like the other kids. If he's smart, he'll weasel his way out of doing the dishes that night, because, he announces, "I don't feel so hot." No one, not even Mom, will call him on that ruse.

No matter what your age or disability, it becomes a game—where and how to play the handicapped card. Even without trying, for instance, you will almost always get seated promptly and with great fanfare at a good restaurant, especially if you've called ahead. If you go there a few more times, you'll end up with a favorite table. Your friends will be impressed and hopefully will want to take you to lunch there.

If you are sitting in an airport baggage line, waiting to get your bags tagged like everyone else, all you have to do, nine times out of ten, to get immediate, head-of-the-line attention is to wheel around all the others and make yourself visible to the skycap. If that doesn't work, make a big issue out of tugging your bag inch by inch; that should engender the sympathy you want. Be sure to tip the guy. He's not doing this to get brownie points in heaven. This also works in movie lines, airport security lines (even with the patting-down, you get through much faster), grocery lines, and an occasional post office line. Where it doesn't work is fast-food lines and ballpark concession stands. Crap food is an equal-opportunity disorder. Just because you're in a wheelchair doesn't mean you need that monster burrito any more or any faster than the next guy.

The decision as to when or when not to demand special consideration is entirely up to the person in the wheelchair. Most people will just assume you deserve it, given the crummy fate you've been handed. Those travelers who need their bags tagged just as quickly as you will quietly grumble when they see you whiz through like the grand pooh-bah you aren't, but they will never say, "Hey, bud, wait your turn." If they do, they'll come across like Mr. Burns on *The Simpsons* and probably incur the wrath of everyone else. "Let him go, man, I mean, jeez ..." You the wheelchair user will feel stupid for becoming the focus of this nonsensical debate, and the airport personnel will immediately try to mollify you. They don't want you showing up in their complaint department with your hard-knuckled disability-rights lawyer and a throng of sign-waving activists.

This check-in scenario is just another of the many tricky social quandaries that color the paralytic's life and test both his self-control and his manners. Do I raise an obnoxious ruckus at the store with the wall-to-wall floor displays or just shop online? Do I chuckle good-naturedly when asked for the zillionth time, loudly, "How's the weather down there?" Do I tell the sister of the lupus survivor at the party to get lost or do I join her support group? When the skycap waves at me, do I zip past the herd, flashing the victory sign, or do I wait my turn? What would the Coronet Film people say?

They'd say that the best thing to do, in most situations, is not to be petty and self-serving, darn the luck. They'd say you should avoid the bad karma of overplaying the disability card. In other words, wait in the baggage line with every other Tom, Dick, and Harry. Will the plane leave without you? No, it won't. Do you really need to jump ahead in the line at the movie and buy your ticket so you can claim your back-row space that the other patrons can't use unless they bring their own folding chairs? No, you don't.

Now please pack up your books and go home.

FIVE

IMMOBILITY AS A CAREER MOVE

IN MY LITTLE DOWNSTAIRS ROOM, there were two main items: the bed and my desktop computer. Everything else besides my family had pretty much been stripped away or minimized, at least during that first year. The computer was a triple threat: a source of endless nonphysical amusement, the best way to communicate with friends, and a means of generating income. I wasn't in solitary confinement, but I often felt as if I were, even with an intact family only a few feet away. I couldn't exactly write mad scribblings on my prison walls to proclaim my innocence or keep myself from going bonkers, but I could do the equivalent on the Etch-a-Sketch surface of the computer screen. Most important, the computer allowed me to work, and work—if anything—looked like the way out of jail.

From Day 1 my impulse was to keep working. As I lay in the hospital, my first phone call after I spoke to my blood relatives and closest friends was to a television producer, Bruce Nash, with whom I had just signed a deal to cowrite a special for the Museum of Television and Radio, about the origins of sitcoms. I wanted to assure him that I was paralyzed, in a complete state of panic, literally pissing in my pants, and crying uncontrollably, but, hey, I was itching to work. "I've got a laptop coming," I said. "Bring me those old Dick Van Dyke tapes. I'm ready to roll."

Looking back, of course, I can see that this was an insane thing to do. If you ever become paralyzed on a weekday afternoon, try to take some time to let the situation soak in. Don't call the office and ask someone to send over your Rolodex. Postpone the order for the new winch you need to extract those tree stumps by the pool. Cancel that appointment with your periodontist; your receding gums can wait.

Most of us don't have the luxury of checking out for six months or more and focusing on this awesome transformation. Franklin Roosevelt, to luxury born, did just that. When he contracted polio in 1921—he was then thirty-nine—he left the wife, the kids, and a tyrannical mother and relocated to the Florida Keys to fish and drink for a couple of years. When that got old, he relocated to Warm Springs, Georgia, to soak in mineral waters and try every other scheme anyone could dream up to help him walk again.

Fearful of a diminished existence, Roosevelt blew a good part of his inheritance pursuing a phantom cure. After helping thousands of paralytics with nowhere else to turn, he

realized that there was more to life than walking. He sub-
sequently reentered public life, was elected president four
times, saved America from the Great Depression, and saved
the world from a bunch of fascist lunatics. But it took him a
good seven to eight years to get back to the office.

I saw professional hara-kiri and financial ruin awaiting
me outside that hospital room if I waited even a week, let
alone seven years. Part of this reaction was simply the manic
message buried deep in my northern European gene pool:
"Work is imperative. Without work, you are a worthless ci-
pher." Part of it was our dire financial situation. But most of
it, I think, was my clearheaded perception of the reality of the
Hollywood workplace: if you stop working, they stop calling.
There are a thousand other worker bees out there to take your
place. The unspoken adage in Hollywood is that if you reach
the age of fifty and you haven't attained a certain station—a
few million in the bank, a TV series job running five or more
years, a brand-name reputation—your odds of making the
big score are just a little worse than your odds of winning the
Pennsylvania "Lucky for Life" lottery. And the end can come
at any time. As the writer Lionel Chetwynd once put it, "You
don't leave Hollywood. Hollywood leaves *you*."

In my own case, I had reached no recognizable high point
in Hollywood, no perch from which I could dabble in show
business without fear of being forgotten or ignored. And I
was paralyzed. Even from Room 5127, I could see that impet-
uous tramp Hollywood packing her bags, taking the keys to
the Camaro, and slamming the screen door on her way out.

Bruce Nash, whom I had met maybe twice, could not have
been kinder when I called him from the hospital. He could
have easily said, "Sounds like you're in bad shape. We'll bring

you in for the next special, I *promise*," which is universal producer patois for "You're screwed, man, I'm hiring a twenty-
four-year-old who never sleeps, and we don't validate." But,
probably against his better judgment, he hung in there.

So the moment I left the hospital, two months after the
initial onset, I had a job to keep me going and make me feel
semi-normal. The trouble was that I couldn't do the job just
by moving four feet from bed to computer. I had to go down
to the studio, navigate a way in and out, and be part of the
production team. For all my bellyaching about wanting to
stay at home and not be bothered by reality, it actually felt
good to go to the office, at least initially. Ann-Marie drove me
back and forth, and my workmates were a lot more focused
on cranking out a show than taking my temperature or feeling my pulse.

In typical freelance fashion, I had barely settled into that
assignment before I started fishing for another one. I was back
to the Hollywood shuffle. The producer Tony Eaton, a friend
of mine, stepped right up. Tony knew all about paralysis; his
college roommate at Berkeley had become a quadriplegic,
and Tony had spent months taking care of him. Tony was
doing an industry award show in Las Vegas and wanted me
to write it. Sinbad would be the host, a personal gofer would
handle every contingency, and I'd be surrounded by a crew of
hardy comrades I'd worked with a dozen times before.

Bruce Nash was not happy when I told him I had to rush
off to Vegas for a long weekend to do another show, which
would have been no problem if I were healthy, which I wasn't.
No one, of course, including me, knew how I would deal
with the obvious strain of being in two places at once. Since
the fact that I was truly paralyzed had yet to sink in, I still

operated in my pre-paralysis Sammy Glick mode. I'd go to Vegas, then work twice as hard on the Nash project when I got back, and at the same time start looking for the next project. If you don't want Hollywood to leave you, never take the bitch for granted.

As we were wrapping up the Vegas show, I was trying to seal the deal on a third project called "Heroic Animals." The freelancer's ideal MO is: finish one, be in the middle of another, start a third. I was saying to myself, "Paralysis, schmalysis, I haven't missed a damn step in this dog race!"

I was clearly, foolishly, over the line. I was Bob Fosse in *All That Jazz*, except that he was taking better drugs and creating masterworks like *Cabaret* and *Lenny* and I was writing punchy copy about heroic beavers.

I finished the taping in Las Vegas late on a Sunday night and got on a plane at 6:30 Monday morning for a meeting in LA. I spent all day writing, bleary-eyed and exhausted, counting the minutes until Ann-Marie came to pick me up. I plopped down in the car, and as she put the wheelchair away, I put my head back and I was gone. I guess you could call it a blackout or a fainting spell, but "psychotic disconnect" or "brain melt" would be closer. Hallucinogenic images and sounds whirled through my head at Mach 14. Time and space disappeared. It was dreamlike, but not a dream. It was dizzying, delirious, brain-scrambling. It felt like what I imagine happens just before you die.

Regaining consciousness, I was dizzy and couldn't breathe. I described the situation to Ann, and she freaked. I saw the look on her face and immediately pronounced myself fine, just a little short of breath, working a little too hard, shouldn't have had that burrito for lunch, got to slow down, etc. She was simultaneously trying to figure out which was the closest ER and repeating, defiantly, "You are not going back to the hospital." I was gasping for air and didn't want to show it. This is called the protection game, a shrink once told me. You protect others dear to you from the truth. You can't breathe a lick, but you try to feign that it's nothing, just a passing air-intake problem.

Not that Ann had discouraged me from getting back to work. We had zero savings and she was wholly dependent on my bread-earning powers. She knew that this process was initially hard on me, but she figured I'd adjust to it in time. She called it a "thread of normalcy." As she later noted, no one at work accommodated me, and I didn't ask for accommodation. As a virgin paralytic, I didn't even know what to ask for. As long as I could fit into the four-by-four-foot elevator to get to the second-floor writers' office, I was there.

Like the rest of us, Ann thought that work was the best medicine for me at the time, plus she was distracted by her own need to find an independent source of income. She immediately signed up for a fast-track credentialing program to enter the LA school district as a full-time teacher. This involved attending classes at Cal State-Northridge and boning up for some tough statewide exams. If I was off to work, fine. She had plenty to do.

After the meltdown that Monday, I took sick leave from every job and lay in bed at home for three days, pretending that I was all right and just needed some rest. By Day 4, when I was preparing to go see an acupuncturist—Dr. Biao Lu—I was still sucking air like a floater. On the way to the appointment, I spilled hot tea all over my baggy gray sweatpants and looked like an incontinent bum. Ironically, we pulled up in front of a homeless shelter next door to Dr. Lu's office; and as I made it from car seat to chair, I abruptly threw up twice, all tea, and then completely blacked out, slumping over like a dead man. I came to again about three inches from the craggy face and beery breath of a fellow transient yelling, "You'll be OK, buddy, you'll be OK," as if he knew.

Ann-Marie quickly rolled me into Dr. Lu's office. Dr. Lu took one look and announced that I needed an emergency dose of western medicine; and in a daze of panic, we went from new age doctor to old age doctor to an oxygen mask in the back of a screaming ambulance to a roomful of shouting doctors at Cedars ER.

I was actually dying, it turned out, from an acute pulmonary embolus (or multiple emboli, to be precise). These were blood clots in the lungs that had traveled up from one of my legs—remember that because of the nonstop work, I had been sitting motionless in a chair for twelve to fourteen hours a day. The clotting had reduced my breathing capacity by about 40 to 50 percent. The right ventricle of my heart had doubled in size, straining to keep me alive. My heart was beating 120 times a minute as it tried to pump unoxygenated blood into my impaired lungs. I was still breathing but had no discernible pulse in my wrist. I guess not much blood was getting to my brain, either—hence the blackouts, not to mention my dim-witted refusal to realize something serious was wrong.

Under astute care and with a steady supply of oxygen, the clots began to dissolve on their own; and in a couple of weeks I was back in the wheelchair, breathing normally but highly attuned to long sitting spells. Something called a Greenfield filter—brilliant contraption—is now implanted in my bloodstream to prevent any clots in my legs from reaching my heart or lungs; the anticoagulant Coumadin keeps me clot-free, I hope. I've had many other health problems growing out of the paralysis, but my heart and lungs seemed to have survived this crisis, which had been induced by my lifestyle and could easily have been avoided.

Not to make too fine a point of it, but I had nearly killed myself trying to maintain my professional front. The attendant Israeli cardiologist put it nicely: "You were one or two clots away from eating it." No one would have said at my funeral, "He died doing what he most loved to do—writing disposable TV shows in order to pay for a house he shouldn't have bought in the first place." No, the honest eulogy would have been: "He was a fool. He thought he was thirty and he was fifty; he thought he was resilient and he was sick; he thought his silly career was more important than his life. How sad is that?"

I was not only facing a financial problem at this juncture; I was facing a character flaw as well, as Ann pointed out more than once. "Your problem," she said, "is that you have always lived more in your brain than in your body." Before, this imbalance only caused headaches, anxiety, and periodic sleep deprivation. Now, ignoring my body involved a serious threat to life and limb, even the paralyzed limbs.

Once the embolism passed, I went right back to working and simultaneously trawling for more work. Paying the mortgage required this, and work did take my mind off my plight and off the self-pity and regret sloshing around in my brain. I had at least learned by this time that if I felt tired, I should stop and lie down for a spell. I had yet to learn to handle dozens of other health risks, but I knew enough to pace myself, exercise to ease the tension of sitting all day, and call in sick when I was sick. In the tussle between body and brain, the body gained a few yards.

I also knew I was no longer seen in the marketplace as a fifty-one-year-old "veteran" writer with a great agent at the Morris office, John Ferriter. I was now a fifty-one-year-old writer "who, you know, just got a horrendous disease or something." At first this didn't seem so bad. A number of check-writing colleagues stepped up to give me work. They probably likened my situation to losing your wife or kicking a cocaine habit. You were damaged, but you clearly needed a break; and by all appearances, you could still do the job. For the first nine months after leaving the hospital, I was gainfully, gleefully employed.

Having never asked, I have no idea if any of the producers or executives who hired me even factored in my condition. My guess is that in most cases I was a good candidate for the job and my ailment contributed a slight edge; it played to their sense of good feeling and generosity. I helped rewrite a terrific TNT documentary about western movies that won a CableAce Award. Even as I took the stage with Len and Georgia Morris, the talented couple who made the film, part of me asked, "Is this because I'm in this wheelchair?" That's totally unfair to both the film and the Morrises, but I felt the helping hand of friends in everything I did that year.

One job was a perfect fit—an all-star Christopher Reeve special on ABC to help launch the Christopher Reeve Foundation. It was a great night, filled with great talent— Stevie Wonder, Willie Nelson, Amy Grant, Robin Williams, and a dozen other celebrities. Christopher Reeve impressed people everywhere, but he was held in especially high regard in Hollywood. He was a fellow performer but, more than that, his life and courage belie the egregious myth that show business is just a bunch of vain, overpaid prima donnas of suspect morals who have no connection to the "real" America. Somehow, when Christopher Reeve appeared, the bitter cultural division between Hollywood and Kansas disappeared.

I kept waiting for *Ironside* to go back on the air so I'd have another inside track, but it didn't happen. A paying job was real therapy, but unfortunately, I didn't have enough friends to feed me a steady diet of work. Between jobs, I became paranoid—"I'll never work again," a typical Hollywood mind-set. But now I was doubly paranoid—"I'll never work again, because I'm damaged goods. Who wants half a writer, for God's sake?" Was Hollywood about to leave me for good? I began a jack story in my head, a suspicion that this disability was the straw that finally broke my professional back. The hyperventilation passed; but the fact is that with few exceptions, I have never been hired in television since I've been paralyzed by anyone I didn't already know before I was paralyzed. And I have not been hired by a lot of people I did know before I was paralyzed.

The blessing of becoming paralyzed at fifty-one is that I had been around for a while, but permanent impairment at any age is not exactly a calling card in the entertainment industry. It's probably not a calling card in the insurance or roofing industries, either; but, unlike roofers, most people in Hollywood trade on their looks and energy. Producers work out like mad, eat wheatgrass, and get their hair dyed to stay young in a youth-obsessed business. Directors wear flashy Australian Outback hats or drive '57 Chevys to secure their maverick image, even as they direct *Return to Gilligan's Island.* Agents, hairdressers, "D-girls"—they all trade on style, flamboyance, savoir faire. And not one of them accessorizes with a wheelchair.

On the other hand, a disproportionate number of people who pay dues to the Writers Guild are fat and sallow, smoke, and dress in sweatpants and Bart Simpson T-shirts. Who cares how they look or smell? Just E-mail the script by Tuesday. In the 1930s writers were described as "schmucks with Underwoods." Change "Underwoods" to "iBooks" and the idea still holds.

Having said this, I should add that there are reputedly only a few working writers in the Writers Guild who are wheelchair users. Why? I have no idea. It's not that disability discrimination in Hollywood is blatant. A budding Robert Towne in a wheelchair can't point to a sign outside Universal reading "The Lame Need Not Apply" and whine about the injustice of it all. It doesn't work like that. Everyone in the workaday world, Universal execs included, is nice to the handicapped. Every person on Sunset Boulevard will help you through a revolving door or direct you to Mr. Big's office.

The discrimination is more habit than hatred. No matter what ambulatory industry types say—"I have never looked on the disabled as anything but normal, regular, everyday people. They don't bother me. They're just people, for gosh sakes!"—hiring someone with a disability, to work in front of or behind the camera, is a big deal. It's probably where hiring African-Americans or Hispanics was in the 1960s. "Hey, look here! We got one! Bill Cosby! He's good, isn't he?"

At least with regard to actors, television in particular not only doesn't hire the disabled, but does a pretty good job of hiding the fact that disabled people even exist. According to a recent study by the Screen Actors Guild, 20 percent of Americans (56 million) have a mental or physical disability, but less than 2 percent of all characters on television shows have a visible disability and only 0.5 percent of disabled characters on these shows have speaking roles. These are fictional characters, not the disabled movie stars who show up at fundraisers and press conferences. Even with all the other doors opening for disabled people these days, from public access to medical research, these statistics are pathetic.

Nevertheless, there are 1,237 self-identified performers in the Screen Actors Guild with disabilities trying to get the three or four available roles. Actors with disabilities are often the gutsiest, and cagiest, people in show business. David Lander, an extremely funny guy who played Squiggy on *Laverne and Shirley*, developed MS in the 1980s and waited a good ten years before he "came out." In his own disease-cum-memoir, *Falling Down, Laughing*, he recounts how he tried to hide his evolving physical symptoms from producers and directors. He would do anything he could—stand behind couches, fidget in character, play in the shadows—to disguise the mild tremor that accompanied his disease. The situation finally came to a head, he says, when he was fired from a play in Chicago for drunkenness at work. What did he do? He shamefully admitted, probably with great thespian verve, to having an alcohol problem. It was better, he figured, to be thought of as a sot than as a person with MS.

There are pitifully few disabled characters on television, but there is at least one prominent disabled actor or celebrity for every major disorder—such as Terri Garr or David Lander for MS, Mary Tyler Moore for juvenile-onset diabetes, and Michael J. Fox for Parkinson's disease—and thank God for each and every one of them. As with Rock Hudson and AIDS, or the veteran Ron Kovic and Vietnam, one highly publicized story is worth a million that never get told. The entertainment press hypes these people as "heroes," which is as debased a term in media culture as "comic genius," "rising star," and "thumbs way up." Heroes, in this context, mean survivors with famous faces who are very skilled at talking about themselves on *Ellen* and *Montel*, especially if doing so can raise a zillion dollars for research.

Celebrity icons help, but the workaday disabled continue to throw a lot of people off their game. The nondisabled probably can't explain it themselves, but there is an X factor that makes them self-conscious, uptight, or embarrassed.

I remember one producer in particular with whom I had spent a good deal of time in the year before I became impaired. I considered him a friend and an all-around good sort. As calls came in to the hospital from well-wishers far and wide, I kept expecting to hear from him. The call never came; nor did a short note; nor did an oversize bouquet of Mylar balloons. I didn't think much of it until about six months later, when it dawned on me that the guy had never gotten in touch. By this point, I was feeling a little better about myself and wanting to renew the connection, so I called him. He immediately started apologizing. I could tell he hadn't forgotten; for all that time, he had been actively not calling. His excuse was that he didn't quite know what to say. I said, "Well, 'How're you feeling?' would have been a good icebreaker." It really wasn't worth discussing. Debilitating illness clearly bothered him, the way a mention of gay sex or electroshock experiments on cats bothers others. He was phobic about it.

This raises a question: is there such a thing as "disability phobia"? Or is it simply in my imagination and the imagination of others like me? It can be a cycle of social miscues: I feel weird because you seem to feel weird because I seem to feel weird because you seem to feel weird because I *am* weird. Now you see why a lot of disabled people never leave the house.

The phobic producer had an extreme reaction, but there are stereotypes out there that linger in the subconscious and muddy the mix. One is the stereotype of the cranky, short-tempered cripple, the Ratso Rizzo in a wheelchair: "Out of my way! I have my rights, you know! This counter is too high. Get me your manager!" Another is the stereotype of the disabled people who expect your help or sympathy at every turn, and if they don't get it, they turn into Ratso: "Could you be so kind as to reach that nonfat peach yogurt way up there? Lady, I'm talking to you. I'm paralyzed, you know."

Touchy or needy. In the 1950s, "needy" was the dominant image. Remember the "Hire the Handicapped" ads on television showing bright-eyed clucks in wheelchairs selling lightbulbs or making straw brooms? Nowadays, "touchy," "irascible," or "pain in the butt" is probably the more apt label. You don't want to hang around paralytics and say or do something that might offend or upset them. They could bite your head off, or at least make you feel guilty.

If any of this is a determining factor in not hiring the disabled—the stigma, the discomfort, the off-putting stereotypes—then it's an old story. The 56 million disabled Americans, arguably the nation's largest minority, are just another maligned subgroup angling for a fair shake. The question is, if I were a producer, would I hire a disabled writer? If I weren't a disabled writer myself, I'd probably hesitate and ponder the downside. "Hey, he's a competent fellow, or at least he was a competent fellow; but, jeez, what if he tires easily? What if he has a medical emergency, like respiratory failure, in the middle of production? It happened once, I hear. What if he, you know, drops dead? That would really bum people out, not to mention put us way behind schedule."

And one more thing—a person in a wheelchair has "special needs"—an accessible hotel room, a ramp to the stage or field office, often a schlepper or his own disabled Porta Potti. Once, when I was arriving in Nashville for a show, the airline announced that they had lost my wheelchair. Somehow it didn't make it onto the plane in LA. Someone had to locate a rent-a-chair in town, get it to me, then hunt down mine and make the exchange. The airline found it in DC the next day, God love 'em; it was being used to transport grannies around Dulles. Hassles abound in this condition. It's built in. And some people don't like the extra baggage, so to speak.

The myth that disabled equals weak equals sick equals unreliable is the myth that dies hardest. Of course, in 2006, disabled means none of those things, which is why there are a plethora of wheelchair marathons, bloodthirsty quad rugby face-offs, para-Olympics, Hawaiian golf tournaments, Adaptive Ski Schools, magazine headlines like "Sex and the Single Para," and a thousand other cultural expressions of disabled strength and vitality. In fact, in today's mass media, disabled equals healthy, risk-taking, and balls-out gutsy. Among disabled people, it's pretty much only these go-getters who ever make the news, which would lead an inveterate television watcher, i.e., most of us, to believe that the whole disabled community is out kayaking or skiing at Aspen. But there is a cultural disconnect somewhere. The handicapped marathoner on TV is one thing; the "normal" guy in the chair in front of you is still a person with a weakness.

This myth is doubly pernicious when it comes to writing as a job. Unlike, say, construction work or selling Bibles door to door, writing is not physically intensive. Good legs aren't required. What was it Yogi Berra said? "Baseball is ninety percent mental—the other half is physical." This also describes writing and a lot of other brain-centric jobs in American industry these days.

This kind of habitual thinking about the disabled is not unique to film and television production. All of American commerce puts a premium on efficiency, productivity, and sixteen-hours-a-day indefatigability. Compassion is a weekend virtue. Just tune in to *The Apprentice*. Or ask a steelworker in Pennsylvania. "Sorry, Pops, your job just moved to Myanmar. Too bad."

Probably the best way to think about this, if you are sitting at home in a wheelchair, is not to think about it at all. No one is ever going to say, "We don't hire people in wheelchairs," just as no one will ever say, "We don't hire fat people" or "We have a firm policy—no Canadians." The less time you spend thinking about your plight, the less self-conscious you will be when you roll into a room for an interview or a pitch, and the less your wheelchair becomes an issue in anyone's mind. If a prospective employer hires you, it doesn't matter. If not, it matters even less. Trust me, you don't want to be around someone who always sees the wheelchair first.

My solution with regard to my own career is a simple, time-tested survival technique I had to use a lot before I became paralyzed. Dance. Stay fluid. Reinvent yourself. Go to where you're wanted, not where you're second-guessed or resented. In my own work situation, after a long period of trial and failure, the picture became pretty clear. Network pitch meetings became a rarity, because I felt out of place and because I wasn't selling anything. I became more of a solo act. Things I could do without leaving the home office—writing special material for a show, researching and writing a documentary, even writing for a website—were more comfortable for me than the creative chaos (and late nights) of group writing or writing on the road. I still write with others—sometimes it's great; sometimes it's weird. Stay away from people who like to move to twelve different writing locations a day.

If you are disabled, you're wearing whatever stigma is attached, or in my case, riding in it, so it will probably always be there in some form. Rudy Giuliani, a big fan of *The Sopranos*, made a very good comment when he was asked to defend the show against all the Italian-Americans who find it degrading and offensive. "Why go around looking for someone to insult you?" he said. A lot of sensitive types, including a lot of sensitive paraplegics, see an insult or affront at every turn. "We decided to go in a different direction"—a very common showbiz line meaning "You're not hired"—could mean "We don't like you," "We don't think you can write worth a lick," or "We don't really want to see a cripple rolling around the office every day, making us feel guilty, sad, or just plain uncomfortable." Of course, maybe it connotes all three, in which case you can just conclude, "They're a bunch of rabid anti-crip-tites," and have a stiff drink. You aren't going to change any minds.

This is all relatively easy for me to say because I don't have one of those jobs demanding the 10 percent physical half of work that Yogi talked about. I was already sitting most of the time, and my silicon-padded wheelchair is easier on my back than the office chair I used to have. I'd been plying the writing trade for about twenty-five years, so I knew the routine and a handful of tricks—I could fake my way through a stage intro for Walter Cronkite or Reba McEntire with aplomb. But one thing was lacking—a sense of urgency. Paralysis added this. It wasn't that writing was something I could still do. It became damn near the only thing I could do. I began to write as though my life depended on it.

For one thing, I couldn't escape it. I could no longer do with ease what most people in my profession do—dick around. Post-paralysis, I had little or no desire to have lunch with other unemployed writers, see every movie that came out, or throw myself into the time-sucking labor of pitching, developing, marketing, and schmoozing for television and film projects. I could still do all those things, of course, but the effort would be much greater. Also, just functioning in a chair brought home something I'd never admitted to myself—I didn't want to do those things. I wasn't itching to go to production meetings, casting marathons, or power breakfasts; and I had never liked being on film sets. Frankly, it's kind of dull. If you're not acting or directing, you're hanging around the snack table, getting fat.

As I became a wheelchair stranger in Hollywood, Hollywood seemed to become a time-wasting stranger to me. Maybe, I started to think, I had made a tragically wrong turn on the 405 freeway thirty-some years ago. Maybe I shouldn't have followed the Hollywood sign to the front door of the

William Morris Agency. Maybe I had never felt that comfortable in this wacko world to begin with.

So I focused, almost by default, on writing. I wrote anything that came to mind—E-mails, journals, letters, lists, story ideas, bad country songs—and I did it every day and felt like a useless slug if I didn't. I just wrote to write. Writing, thank God, has no start-up costs. Like Jack Nicholson in *The Shining*, you just do it obsessively, even if it is the same line over and over again.

According to a remembrance in the *New Yorker* by Richard Ford, the late short-story writer Raymond Carver had a pet phrase to describe what it took to be a serious writer. It wasn't talent; that was just an unquantifiable something that many seem to have and few exploit. "What delivers," Ford concluded, "was 'being at your station,' as Ray said: being there, present to do the work." Nothing better describes the endless hours I wrote in a vacuum and to no end in my little room than "being at your station." It was largely because I didn't know what else to do, but it was something, and it kept me marginally sane.

At the time, I didn't know how scared I was. Putting on a brave front for myself as much as for anyone else and throwing myself into face-saving monkey work didn't help much. Habitual writing did. And doing it, day in and day out, had an almost biochemical effect. Writing, in short, gave me courage.

The writer Adam Smith once called sports the "American yoga." My guess is that America's yoga is closer to watching football on television or genuflecting at the speaker box at McDonald's, but the point is this: America's yoga is probably not yoga. We all yearn to find a concentrated activity that draws us into at least a temporary state of unconscious well-being. Hugh Hefner found sex. Ann Coulter found Joe Mc-Carthy. Lance Armstrong found embarrassing the French. On the wrong side of fifty, I found that the activity of writing had many more benefits than just being a livelihood. If I knew that before, I had never sat still long enough, so to speak, to appreciate it.

SIX

JOINING THE PPA—PARALYZED PEOPLE OF AMERICA

SOMETIME IN THE MIDDLE OF that first year, I told myself that I could handle this cruel malady, and I almost believed it. I could comport myself in public with a modicum of dignity, I could keep up my health, and I could even earn a living—as long as the paralysis was a temporary imposition, of course. All my cheerfulness and can-do-ism rode on the assumption that, little by little, I would recover, and that my recovery would propel me like a second-stage booster rocket into a satisfying post-paralysis life. I couldn't wait to see my nerves down there spring slowly back to life. I couldn't wait to make walking my new hobby.

I remained fitfully confused and depressed—even temporary paralysis is seriously disorienting—but at least hope had a fighting chance. There was absolutely no reason on earth why I wouldn't recover. I figured that a combination of time, good nutrition, and a PMA (positive mental attitude) would do the trick. No one had told me I *wouldn't* recover, so I assumed that I would and that when it finally happened, everyone on my health team would be greatly relieved and salute me in unison.

As I waited for this inevitable comeback, I began to wonder about the whole big community of wheelchair users. Away from the hospital, I didn't bump into a lot of them. If you go mall-cruising on a Saturday afternoon, at least in LA, you won't see many wheelchairs. This started to bother me. I'd go tooling around LA's Westside Pavilion and feel as though I were in a science fiction movie where I was the last crippled person on earth. In my head, I could hear the alien commander fuming, "What? You let one escape? Confound it, Beldar, find him and bring him to the *Death Star*, now!" I kept wondering, Where are all the other wheelchair users? Who are all the other wheelchair users? I wanted to know something about the membership of this club I'd been asked to join, even as a temporary associate.

Actually, I was a new member in a couple of clubs. First there was the select Transverse Myelitis Club, a group as diverse as the whole spectrum of humanity. Transverse myelitis is considered a specific disorder, not just a clump of symptoms; but there is huge variation in the extent of damage, the consistency and duration of immobility, and whatever cause might be detected. According to Sandy Siegel, president of the Transverse Myelitis Association (TMA), it can strike people as young as four months and as old as eighty-five years. Children, in fact, make up about 28 percent of the approximately 33,000 people in the United States believed to have TM. I have yet to run across someone who exactly mirrored my own case, but he's probably out there—a fifty-one-year-old male in excellent physical if not mental health, blindsided for life.

According to Sandy, TM is an old diagnosis, dating back to the turn of the twentieth century but apparently kept as a closely held secret among physicians for years. When Sandy's wife, Pauline, then a kindergarten teacher in her mid-thirties, fell down on the floor of the bathroom in excruciating pain in July 1994, TM was virtually unknown to the lay public. At the start-up meetings of the TMA in 1995, Sandy met people who had had TM for twenty or thirty years but who had never met anyone else with the disease. The association has gone from 150 to almost 6,000 members in ten years, publishes a newsletter, and runs a very informative website but still has no paid employees. It's hard to sustain a national advocacy group from such a small universe of cases. Transverse myelitis does have at least one celebrity advocate, Cody Unser, daughter of racing legend Al Unser, Jr., two-time Indianapolis 500 winner. Cody contracted TM at age twelve and now, at eighteen, impressively runs her own foundation to promote the cause of stem cell research to help cure her disorder.

Once you acquire TM and the inflammation subsides and you know the true nature of the damage, you're pretty much like any other person with a spinal cord injury (SCI). You have all the same problems to deal with—pain, spasticity, bladder and bowel dysfunction, and systemic infection, to name a few—and you're likely to be given the same treatment options. What this meant was that I was automatically added to the rolls of a much bigger club: all those Americans who had some kind of SCI. I thought the numbers would be in the millions, as with lung cancer (more than 170,000 new cases a year) or Parkinson's disease (50,000 new cases a year), but I was wrong. According to a very reliable source, the National SCI Statistical Center in Birmingham, Alabama, the annual incidence of spinal cord injuries of any kind is approximately 40 cases per million, or some 11,000 new cases a year. I was surprised to discover that in the United States the total population with SCIs is "only" about 250,000, give or take a few thousand. If you are one of those 250,000, it's a central fact of your existence; but in the universe of popular diseases, it doesn't hold a candle to breast cancer, adult-onset (or type 2) diabetes, or Alzheimer's, any of which affects millions. Type 2 diabetes alone affects more than 14 million people in the United States. That's a big club.

Maybe I thought there were a lot more paralytics out there because they are overrepresented in the popular media—or at least a few, like disabled athletes and other luminaries, are overrepresented. Paralysis is a media-friendly disorder. It has instant visual and emotional impact. It is often associated with events we like to watch on television: drive-by shootings, pro football, motorcycling racing and other daredevil sports, the ravages of war, and ten-car pileups on the 405. Who over forty has forgotten the 1982 car crash that put R&B great Teddy Pendergrass in a power chair? There was also the highly publicized case of the New England Patriots' receiver Darrel Stingley, paralyzed for life by a perfectly legal blow dealt by Oakland Raider Jack Tatum. Years later, Tatum lost a leg from the complications of diabetes, but no one remembers that. It's not something you can replay on *Sports Center* a million times.

Let's face it, paralysis, whether it involves a kid on a local hockey team who gets cracked in the back or a soldier rolling down the gangplank of a C-130 transport, makes good TV. (Given the roughly 15,000 soldiers wounded in the Iraq war as of late 2005, there are plenty of brand-new wheelchair users in the news.) Unlike heart disease or cystic fibrosis, you can *see* paralysis—it can't be hidden or disguised—and it's rarely a precursor of physical death. You don't "beat" it, like cancer—you live with it. In most cases, it's a cruel fate that happens, often out of the blue, to someone who was doing something we all could be doing—driving a car, playing a sport, falling off the roof while fixing the chimney. You don't have to smoke too many cigarettes or eat too many double bacon cheeseburgers to get it. War aside, it's usually an accident, like stubbing your toe, only worse.

If paralysis happens to a celebrity or star athlete, the coverage is wall-to-wall. By the time I became paralyzed, Christopher Reeve, paralyzed two years earlier, had made spinal cord injury almost a daily news event. Most people had never seen a quadriplegic in a wheelchair on TV before, except for perhaps a quick shot of the physicist Stephen Hawking or a spunky kid wheeled out during the Jerry Lewis telethon or some other heart-tugging charity function. They'd certainly never seen one center stage at the Oscars, respirator in tow; or speaking forcefully before Congress; or being interviewed by Barbara Walters, Oprah Winfrey, and every other pundit west of Bill O'Reilly.

In his tragically short stint as the world's most famous paralytic, Christopher Reeve got a lot of people talking about spinal cord injuries. He popularized the once unimaginable notion that paralysis might be cured and helped rally broad public support for finding a cure through stem cell research. In a few years he became a mediagenic symbol and common link between all people with central nervous system (CNS) disorders—a club with ranks in the tens of millions. The story may be apocryphal, but I read somewhere that Mr. Reeve had single-handedly raised more money for medical research than any other individual in the history of fundraising. Aside from FDR, paralysis has never had a bigger public light than Christopher Reeve.

But Christopher Reeve doesn't really fit the profile of the average person with SCI, I soon learned. Most people who become paralyzed are not established celebrities or equestrians. Also, SCI is largely a young man's malady. Statistically, the average age of injury in 2000 was around thirty-eight, up from 28.6 in 1979. This rise is attributable, no doubt, to a general rise in age of the whole population led by the dreaded baby boomers. A distinct majority of those injured—78.2 percent—are male, and the most common cause (50.4 percent) is a car accident. This is followed by falls, acts of violence (mostly gunshot wounds), and recreational sporting activities. Fifty-three percent of these car-driving or gun-shooting or jet-ski-riding young men are single at the time of their accident.

And as you might guess, the rate of alcohol and drug abuse among these young guys in wheelchairs is high—nearly 50 percent, compared with a rate of 10 to 15 percent in the general population. Of course a lot of these people drank or used drugs before they became paralyzed, and since over 50 percent of them got injured in car accidents, there's a good chance they were drinking or flying at the time. The quadriplegic cartoonist John Calahan, as he accounted in his book *Don't Worry—He Won't Get Far on Foot*, had to deal with paralysis and chronic alcoholism at the same time. He probably has plenty of company.

I often wonder how much harder it must be for someone starting out in life to confront the barriers of this condition, compared with, say, a fifty-one-year-old writer with a wife, two kids, and a union health plan. There's a whole new generation defying these barriers, but it's got to be tough for most young-and-paralyzed to be macho in a wheelchair or to go clubbing or push your way through a crowded bar to woo some beauty. It's tough to windsurf with your girl, assuming you can find one who can handle your condition, play softball with your office mates, or golf with your boss. And it is no doubt especially tough for anyone that age to admit that they have continence and/or erectile dysfunction problems.

Thinking about this, I almost felt blessed to be middle-aged and paralyzed, as stupid as that sounds.

A fine club, the Brotherhood of Paralysis, but I didn't want to be a part of it for one minute longer than necessary. I was itching to move on, and rather than just waiting for a cure, I thought that maybe I could nudge it along with a little out-of-the-box thinking. So, at the suggestion of a parent at Max's school, I turned to the wise counsel and sharp needles of Dr. Lu, my acupuncturist for the next year.

Dr. Lu was an extremely open and generous man, a lot

more engaging, frankly, and a hell of a lot more optimistic about cures and remedies than anyone I'd met at Cedars-Sinai. Dr. Lu examined me with only his fingers and his instincts about illness and health, and gave me a novel explanation of my troubles. His theory was that my immune system hadn't been able to function because of my lifelong refusal to let it respond naturally. I had kept my poor immune system locked in solitary confinement without proper exercise time. Consequently, it was wound up like a spring, ready to pounce on any biological enemy that crossed its path. A virus showed up in the wrong place and the spring went whammo! up and down my spinal column. It didn't just attack the virus. It beat it to death. The spine went down.

Dr. Lu summed up my condition by saying that my body had "too much wind and too much wetness." I didn't have the foggiest idea what he was talking about—it clearly wasn't about flatulence or water retention—but I tried to marry his wiggy diagnosis to my own self-assessment. Bad work habits, I calculated, and bad thoughts about yourself = life out of balance = too much internal wind and moisture = immune suppression = horrible physical deformity.

The imagery baffled me, but the general notion sounded reasonable. I had let stress, anxiety, and inflated ambition force a bodily reaction that involved, unfortunately, the non-regenerating nerves of the spine. Every thought has a biological repercussion, and vice versa, according to Deepak Chopra and a lot of other mind-body specialists. I had worried myself paralyzed. I let an early-childhood narcissistic disturbance misdirect my life and ruin my health. How could I be so stupid?

The problem with this analysis is that there is not one whit of medical evidence to back it up. The effects of stress, overwork, and self-centeredness are surely detrimental to a healthy life, but any connection between these psychological conditions and T-10 paralysis has yet to be made. Either Dr. Lu is way, way ahead of the game—a common belief among Westside LA alt-med types—or he was simply spinning an elaborate metaphor to nudge me into slowing down and taking my life, and my health, more seriously. Or, third, he's completely full of baloney.

I went with Door #1—that he was onto something that had yet to make it on the western medical agenda. Bill Moyers had just done a much-ballyhooed PBS special on Chinese medicine, and I am easily swayed by anything I see on TV. I started seeing Dr. Lu twice a week and subjecting myself, happily, to needle insertions up and down my spine, in my neck, and down my lifeless legs. I also drank his herbal tea remedies, which tasted like liquid dirt, and often left his Santa Monica office with a needle sticking out of the top of my head. I wore a hat to cover it up. More than once, I asked myself why I was doing all this, especially the pinhead routine. What was this? Some form of Chinese penitence for a wet and windy interior? Was the needle akin to a medieval hair shirt, there to constantly remind me that I am a sinner and need to change my ways, as if the wheelchair weren't reminder enough?

I really didn't put these or many other questions directly to Dr. Lu. I submitted to his treatment with only one goal in mind: muscle response. I am far from being an expert in the benefits of acupuncture—or even *Newsweek*-level knowledgeable—and I never felt I needed to be. I just wanted to use acupuncture, either as a legitimate therapy or as a rank, wishful-thinking placebo, to get moving again. I was looking for quick, easily verifiable, concrete evidence. This had absolutely nothing to do with feeling better or even feeling better about myself. The truth is that Dr. Lu's treatments, even the needle in the cranium, were incredibly relaxing and tension-relieving. But I wasn't interested in a weekend at the Golden Door. If he had hit me in the head with a ball-peen hammer and my left leg had jumped, that would've been fine with me. I wasn't into the idea of eastern medicine. I was into cold, hard results.

I had avoided any kind of formal counseling or therapy since becoming paralyzed. I had had some bad luck with talk therapy before—seven years of bad luck, to be exact—and I figured that no ambulatory therapist could understand what I was going through. If I had any therapeutic assistance, it came from Dr. Lu. In his soft, reassuring way, he told me three things that have stuck with me. The first is simple: when you feel like crying, you should go off by yourself and cry. Don't hold the anguish in; don't make it a public event.

Second, he said, we all must find a ritual or practice to eliminate the boundaries that our minds impose. These boundaries are "crippling" (his word), and they obscure our connection to our greater self, which in reality is a connection that is not hard to make. This is a kind of elementary Buddhism or maybe Taoism, but the timing was right—my mind at the time was building boundaries by the carload. The operative word here is "practice." It's not necessarily prayer, meditation, or reading scripture, the usual suspects. He left it at that.

Finally, he said, "we believe"—the way he started every such pronouncement—that negative events always produce positive ones and positive events invariably produce negative ones. There is an inevitable rebalancing. That's why, in his view, people who get many positive things handed to them in life should be wary. No matter how secure, or smug, they feel, there are less pleasant events on the horizon to redress the imbalance. (This smacks a little of schadenfreude to me— delighting in the prospect of someone's downfall—but in a goofy place like Hollywood, where you see modestly talented people getting ridiculously rich and famous on a daily basis, it's a comforting thought.)

I didn't for a moment believe that my life would be magically rebalanced; but if you're newly paralyzed and freaked out in general, it's always good to hear someone tell you that a new harmony is in your future. Dr. Lu ended this conversation by adding one last sunny prediction: emotionally if not physically, my situation would get worse before it got better. I thought, How much worse could it get? "Thanks, Dr. Lu, please take this pin out of my head—I gotta go."

Along with the sessions with Dr. Lu, I also started a rigorous outpatient rehab routine at Daniel Freeman Hospital in Inglewood, a suburb of LA. This made a lot more common sense to me than Dr. Lu's theories and needles. It took recovery out of the realm of emotional or spiritual resuscitation and into the realm of athletic conditioning, something I could grasp. Athletics invites you to set a physical goal—finish a marathon, say, or serve up a tennis ball at 100 miles per hour—and then asks you to muster the discipline and resolve to reach it. You don't sit around thinking about training for a marathon; you just do it, as the ad says. In my case, the athletic program involved stretching—and being stretched—and bending and grunting and making a sweat-drenched effort to move my legs without friction or gravity. Also, you keep doing the program even when nothing is happening. The theory is that if there is any nerve connection whatsoever down there, then by God you're going to do everything possible to get a message through. And what the hell, even if you don't, you've had a good stretch.

Around Day 128—I kept the "hostage crisis" numbers game up well into the 300s—I was working out with Herlene McLees, my indefatigable rehab specialist, and the earth stood still. Actually, the earth moved, in the form of my left leg, then my right. I could move both of them, ever so slightly, in one or two areas. Now we were finally getting somewhere.

"On Day 128," I wrote down, "I am no longer a paraplegic. I am a recovering paraplegic. I can now move, without gravity or friction, three, count 'em, three separate muscles! The flexor, at the top of the thigh, good for moving the thigh forward while lying on my side. The quad, good for moving the lower part of the leg forward, same position. And, today, the hamstring, good for moving the lower leg back. Sitting up and leaning way back, with my legs flopped over the side of the mat, I can now bring my lower leg up a few inches and then hold it there. It doesn't sound like much, but it is. It's a sign of life."

We're talking about inches here, with a lot of straining and grunting, but every slight flex brought tears to my eyes. That same day, Ann-Marie and I were leaving the hospital when we saw a bag-lady-in-training in a dilapidated old clunker with a bumper sticker reading, "God has been GOOD to me!" My cynical response was that I knew a hundred people God had been better to than this poor soul. Then I thought, Hey, maybe God has been good to *me*; I was weathering this awful storm.

The focus of my life became the two little muscle areas: the top of the thigh and the quad in front. Only under optimal conditions—no gravity, no friction, lying down or sitting up with my back leaning way back—could I get any movement. And the movement was fractional. Sometimes, in the optimal lying position, I'd start moving my leg forward, straining like a pig in quicksand, and the weight of the leg would continue the swing for another 90 degrees. This was cheating, but I counted it anyway. I mean, who the hell was keeping score but me?

I was also introduced to water, the best way known to man to exercise a weak paralytic muscle. When you are bobbing in the water with a flotation device or holding onto the side of the pool, there is no friction or gravity. Of course it was difficult for a klutz like me to physically get into the pool, especially the one at our home, which had cinder-block siding. But you figure this stuff out and go on. Swimming is great. A pool is the only other environment besides the bed where I feel perfectly normal.

These isolated muscle responses were all I needed to see my physical life in a positive frame, just as I saw it when Dr. Rovner had said there was a chance of remission. If anyone else involved felt otherwise, from Herlene to Dr. Lu, they didn't say anything. Like an Oscar-winner, I gave credit to everyone in sight—East and West, pins in the head and positive thinking, too much wind and tedious leg exercises—and waited for the next breakthrough. I was hoping, of course, that further movement would involve some non-walking areas of my lower body just a few inches down the road from the flexor muscle that could move my thigh. I mean, there are other fun things to do south of the belly button besides walk and kick footballs.

I was fully cognizant that this restoration of nerve function might take some time, so nine months into the "recovery," I figured that I should bite the bullet and learn how to drive without using my feet. Daniel Freeman had a training program for disabled drivers, so I signed up. The driving is done with hand controls mounted on the steering column, and at first blush it seems simple enough. There is a lever installed next to the turn signal—you move it one way (down) to accelerate and another way (forward) to brake. Child's play, right? Not if you have spent the preceding thirty-five years driving a car with your right foot and often your left elbow (good while eating a cheeseburger). Your previously learned responses are all screwy. Again, you're starting over. After you've mistakenly pushed the lever to brake in the middle of an intersection or pulled it down to accelerate into the garage door, you realize, Hey, this new hand-to-brain routine is harder than I thought. To me, it gave a new meaning to the "disabled" placards hanging on some rearview mirrors. It now meant: Watch out—this yokel may run over your foot.

I remember the day I went down to the DMV to take my hand-control driving test. The tester regaled me with horror stories of people she saw who had no clue about what they were doing. She pointed to a huge hole in a hedge that a handicapped man had driven through a few days earlier. He had just had his hand controls installed and hadn't gotten the hang of them yet—in fact, he had never used them before. She also told me there were dozens, if not hundreds, of people driving around the LA freeways who were paralyzed but had no hand controls—after all, controls cost about $2,000 to $3,000, installed; and the driving lessons cost $400 to $500. "How do they drive?" I asked. "Any way they can," she said. "They use broom handles, walking canes, fire pokers, baseball bats, golf clubs, you name it. They've got one hand on the wheel, hopefully, and the other jamming the stick at the accelerator or brake pedal. And they're usually old."

That image has haunted me ever since: some old coot in a rusted-out Buick poking a nine iron blindly at the foot pedals, hoping he hits the right one just before he bashes head-on into me going sixty miles an hour.

During the first year no doctor or rehab person would give me any prediction as to my recovery, for obvious reasons. It's a no-win situation for them. In the end, they look either Pollyannaish or mean. "You're sure to walk again" sounds like your mother saying, "You can do anything you put your mind to." "You'll never walk again" sounds like your dad saying, "You'll never amount to squat." Plus, who the hell knows? Everyone would throw around vague time frames for pronounced recovery: six months, twelve months, eighteen months. You, the paralytic, will naturally seize on the biggest window you can find to keep hope alive. On top of that, I had real movement! Certainly some movement naturally leads to more movement. Certainly a flexor twitch today means a knee or ankle twitch tomorrow. Right?

At the time I didn't know something that was recently reported in *Frontiers in Bioscience 9* (a magazine you probably don't have lying around the house), that recovery generally begins in six months—that's what happened to me, kind of—

and "the vast majority of patients show some restoration of neurologic function within eight weeks," which didn't happen to me. Also, recovery "may be rapid during months three through six after symptom onset."

The muscle response I described earlier is the only muscle response that has ever returned. That was it. No matter how many needles Dr. Lu stuck in my back and no matter how many leg-strengthening and range-of-motion exercises I did at Daniel Freeman Hospital, nothing else happened. I can still move those same two or three muscles today, eight years later, in a friction-free environment like a swimming pool. And it still feels great. But, as yet, there's nothing else to report response wise, and unless I make Transverse Myelitis history, there never will be.

Around Day 334, close to the end of the first year, I decided to search out a second opinion. I visited a well-known neurologist at the UCLA Medical Center who I hoped would give me a more upbeat assessment than the vague and noncommittal ones I was getting from Dr. Rovner and others. After checking out my medical records and MRI tests, this expert's assessment was hardly encouraging. He had no emotional investment in either me or my disease, so he didn't mince words. I can't remember what he said well enough to quote him exactly; but I fully remember how I felt as I left his office and rolled back to the parking garage. I felt paralyzed for life.

Here's what I absorbed, for the first time: "You're screwed, bud. Your chances of recovery are zip and it will be years or decades or never before western medicine can help you in any way." I do remember the doctor saying that every case is different and ordering up a new MRI, but he wasn't fooling anyone, especially me. I know "forgetaboutit" when I hear it.

The new MRI only confirmed his assessment. The nerve damage now reached from T-10 downward to T-12 and was much more extensive than originally anticipated. The best-case scenario, he thought, was that I'd get just enough nerve restoration and muscle response to perhaps walk again with waist-to-toe leg braces. Having tried full-size leg braces in rehab and feeling like Frankenstein's gawkier brother, this prospect didn't exactly light my fuse. The wheelchair seemed like a much easier if not more dignified way of getting around.

I cried, in private, as Dr. Lu said, and I felt worthless and defeated for days on end; but the intense suicidal grief and devastation I was bracing for never came. Killing myself never presented itself as a plausible option. Perhaps I had already known my fate for months, on some level, and this doctor had just been the first to say it out loud, without sugarcoating. The word "recovery," I now realized, had been slyly dropped from the official conversation since around month six. I think the strategy at Cedars was to let the reality of the situation come to me gradually, allowing me as much time as possible to adjust. Given my well-documented professional naïveté about preparing for the future, it would have taken a good three or four years for this reality to sink in. Remember that I was still counting on "making it" in showbiz after thirty years of not doing so.

There could be another explanation for my tempered response—that I flat-out didn't believe the guy. How could I possibly spend the rest of my life in this wheelchair? It didn't compute. If I had been shot in the back or had gotten scrunched in a nasty car wreck, sure. But you don't just sit up one day with a sharp pain in your side and end up paralyzed for life. You go through a year or two of hell, sure, but it can't keep on forever. Only a fatalist would believe that—or someone, God forbid, who just gave in to being paralyzed, for whatever sick reason. These doctors don't know shit, I kept reminding myself; they have a name for this thing, but not much else. The day I walk again, they'll all gather around and say, "Hmm, that's interesting—let's write this one up for *Frontiers in Bioscience 10*."

Another thing that dawned on me, perversely, was that a prognosis of no-change-for-life meant that I would now be forced to adjust to the existence of a common, everyday wheelchair user. The Grand Adventure of a sudden, cataclysmic, life-altering illness was over. Along with all the pain and humiliation, there had been a heightened reality that bordered on addictive. Becoming paralyzed is high drama: your life is seemingly in the balance; every moment is new; doctors are arguing over what to do next; your whole being is charged. Not unlike war or bullfighting, I guess, it's a peak experience—you are totally alive. I was looking for the same charged drama, the same hormonal rush, at the other end of my "Paralyzed Like Me" saga, the walking end. How exhilarating would it be to walk across a room, however bumblingly, after months, if not years, confined to a wheelchair? That wasn't going to happen now. Ten years into the future, I now knew, I'd be getting up in the morning the same way, wheeling around the house and bumping into doorways the same way, living with all the same tedious irritations of paralysis. Where's the drama in that?

As the second year of my new life began, I decided to end the absurdly optimistic "hostage crisis" day count. I was still looking, though weakly, for some magical change, but I could no longer maintain the pretense that it was just a matter of days before the captives would be freed and would scurry into the arms of their loved ones. The broadest window of recovery I had heard at the time was eighteen months. This meant I still had a good six months to turn things around. But that was only half of my brain talking; the other half knew I was bullshitting myself. The year of hope was over. The little shop of miracles had closed for business. I was crippled, probably for life; and that, said the cat, was that.

SEVEN

HOW'S THE FAMILY?

DR. LU WAS RIGHT ABOUT one thing: by year two, things had gotten a whole lot worse. The psychological numbness and novelty of becoming paralyzed had worn off, and an ugly new gestalt set in. I guess that's how these things go, though I didn't know it at the time. You figure that you will get through one year of sadness, depression, self-pity, anger, confusion, shame, and resentment, and then it'll be smooth sailing. This is the new normal, right? You've lived with it for a year—you can live with it for a lifetime. Not true. You don't just adapt and go on. It's a bit like an emotional tsunami. The water goes way, way out and things seem calm. Then you return to sunning on the beach, close your eyes, and relax; and the floodwaters come rushing back when you least expect them and drown you in a deeper despair. Cheap metaphor, but you get the idea.

One common explanation of the effects of marijuana is that it is a heightener: it amplifies whatever you are feeling or thinking at the time. If you are ready to kick back and have a few laughs, getting stoned will kick you way back and the stupidest things will seem hilarious. If you are depressed or anxious, you will probably find yourself even more so after the initial buzz. If you're hungry, of course, you gorge like the fat man at the pie-eating contest.

Paralysis is also a heightener. It first heightens your sensitivity to your physical presence in the world and how other people respond to that presence. That is what motivates the grouchy cripple—he or she overreacts to the slightest indication of presumed disrespect or disregard. Wheelchair users have been known to slash the tires of cars illegally parked in the blue-striped handicapped zone. It's what you might call a roll-by slashing, which is only a couple years in prison away from a drive-by shooting. That's an overreaction, for sure, but when you are as sensitive as an overweight, pimply-faced fifteen-year-old about every little slight, insult, or challenge to your personal authority as a human being, you do a lot of overreacting. "Mom, please, if I want to pierce my nipple, I'll pierce my nipple, OK? And you can't stop me!"

If phase one of this paralysis saga—the long hospital stay—was like a second infancy, and phase two—the first year—was like a second stint in grade school, that is, learning how to behave in the world, then phase three—lasting two years for me—had all the markings of an anxious, nail-biting second adolescence. You don't really know who you are. You are moody and indecisive. You can't figure out how to cut your hair or what to wear to school. You are often petulant, demanding, sarcastic, and looking for a fight. And who does an adolescent fight with the most?

His family.

More central to your life than being dissed at the mall is the way an illness like this heightens all the problems within your family that you've been so good at masking and sidestepping for years, if not decades. If you've done a good job of putting everyone at home under stress before you landed in a wheel-chair, they're all going to be under red-letter stress afterward. In general, though, this factor doesn't necessarily show up in divorce statistics. Since most SCI victims are single when they become paralyzed, the comparative divorce rate post-paralysis isn't as high as you might think. But there are plenty of other signposts. The rates of substance abuse, unemployment, and depression—all roughly three times the national percentages among nondisabled people—point to the ability of paralysis to exacerbate family tensions already stewing.

Our family had a fair amount of thorny "issues" germinat-ing in the cellar of our too-big house long before December 10, 1996. Some of these very private problems don't bear repeating here; this isn't the Bill Clinton or Jane Fonda story, after all, and I'm not trying to satisfy your need for titilla-tion or to "set the record straight." Unlike Jane, I didn't go to Hanoi, I have no famous father to defame, and, sadly, I have no ménage à trois to confess. But aside from such laundry-airing, the Sturm und Drang in our family during those first few years was probably the most sustained soap opera within the soap opera. If sudden-onset paralysis is high drama, the fallout among your closest relations is low, drip-drip drama, the painful, relentless kind, the kind that Dr. Phil and mar-riage counselors and Lifetime Cable movies trade in.

We were, as Dr. Phil might phrase it, "in pain," but no "changing days" seemed to be on the horizon. We weren't ready, at that point, to "get real!" Specifically, Ann-Marie and I had a two-person struggle on our hands; and the rest of the clan—Blaine, in college; Max, in middle school; and Agda, Ann-Marie's Swedish-born mother, who lived with us—each had their own moments of emotional collapse. It seemed to be contagious, like a flu that gets passed around the house. The difference is that flu disappears after a few days of watching daytime TV. This took years.

Given our precarious financial situation, money seemed to dominate a lot of the husband-wife spats from the start, once death and disfiguration were off the table. Ann-Marie's initial fear, for good reason, was being left out in the cold: no husband; two kids and an aging mother to care for; no job; and a pile of debt. We were never flat broke, often thanks to some timely loans from dear friends and relatives, but we were constantly juggling, recalculating, and fretting. We never missed a mortgage payment—after a revision of terms with the mortgage company—and we stayed on top of our college loan for Blaine. We were just in a hole we had dug long before the paralysis hit that was only made worse by its obvious costs, emotional and financial. The constant worry was like a fly buzzing in your ear—you keep slapping at it, and one month you even kill it, but then its brother shows up two weeks later. It's the endless struggle that millions of Americans with their average $7,000 credit card balance deal with every day. The paralysis just added an ugly new twist.

We had good health insurance—thank you, Jesus—but we were always worried that maybe some huge slice of my medical costs might not be covered. We knew we weren't covered for such necessities as ramps, special bathroom fixtures, automotive hand controls, or anything else mechanical that might make life in a wheelchair more livable. We were always worried that there was something else we had overlooked, something a lot more costly than a grab bar.

The other shoe dropped about three months into the ordeal. At eight o'clock one Tuesday morning, I got a call from a very sweet-voiced worker in the Cedars-Sinai billing department. Her exact words were: "Mr. Rucker, beyond what your insurance covers, you owe us a balance of $109,000. How will you be paying for that—check or credit card?"

My heart sank. Not knowing the murky world of health care accounting, I assumed I owed that amount, since the hospital said so, and only through bankruptcy would it go away. In their continuing coverage of what they call America's health crisis, television news shows tend to focus on, say, a poor family in Alabama completely ruined by one child's catastrophic illness and the sixteen uncovered trips to Johns Hopkins in search of a cure. It happens a lot, I guess; millions of Americans are one health crisis away from total ruin. In the wake of that call, I was sure it had just happened to me.

A week later I developed the pulmonary embolism that took me to death's door. Coincidence? Hard to say.

Once I got out of the hospital after the embolism, I had no choice but to fight it out with Cedars over their blood money. With the help of three or four experts in my corner, we got to the root of the issue, which, like a lot of health costs, was a bureaucratic dispute between the hospital and the insurance company's accountants. The $109,000 bill turned out to be the cost of my extended stay in the rehabilitation wing of the hospital, which to me was just "the hospital." Apparently

Blue Cross Insurance doesn't cover long-term rehabilitation expenses; in their goofy, catch–22 universe, rehabilitation from sudden-onset paralysis isn't a "medical" necessity. I guess they think it's just a fun thing to do while waiting to freak out and be moved to the psycho wing.

Two years and a mountain of useless paperwork later, the whole matter somehow got worked out between two giant computers in the two accounting departments and I finally stopped getting monthly dunning notices with "We're Going to Take Your House!" or some such fear tactic on the envelope. I actually have no idea how it got resolved. Maybe some bill processor somewhere just felt sorry for me and hit "delete" on his keyboard. I ended up paying about $1,000 and the case was closed.

My health was just as precarious as our finances. For the first two to three years—and to this day, actually—there was always the edgy expectation that some unknown side effect would pop up. Because I initially did such a poor job of even the most elementary preventive practices, like caring for skin breaks and pressure sores, I made numerous trips to the ER with a fever of 103 to 104 degrees. Since I couldn't feel the pain of the fever-causing infection coming, the thermometer was my only clue. And since I cringed at the idea of making another depressing Sunday-night trip to the ER, I tended to wait until my temperature reached a range well beyond what would be caused by a sore neck muscle. In a way, every trip was like the very first trip, when for ninety minutes I assumed I had a bad case of flu—until I crumpled to the floor.

During the first three years of paralysis, I spent a cumulative three months or more at Cedars-Sinai, usually staying three or four days per visit. At one point I went in for an infection in my leg, and Dr. Norman Lavet, who was then my internist, happened to hear a strange sound in an artery in my neck while doing a routine stethoscope check. It turned out that my right carotid artery, the big one just to the right of the Adam's apple, was 95 percent blocked with plaque. An immediate incision and clean-out job was needed, and the OR was notified.

You have two carotid arteries taking blood to your brain, thank goodness, so I wasn't being deprived of brain blood; but this was major surgery and perhaps an indication of arterial problems in the future. Still in a postoperative fog, I felt compelled to ask: what did this condition and the operation, called an endarterectomy, have to do with my paralysis? As far as anyone could tell, nothing. More important, what would have happened if Dr. Lavet hadn't stumbled across that blockage? A loose piece of plaque could have floated upward into my brain and caused a stroke. Oh, no, I thought, not the stroke ward again.

Periodic scares like this would be enough to keep anyone on edge. But beyond health and money, The Big Issue in our home was the future. After thirty years of marriage, my wife and I didn't appear to have one. We had been kidding ourselves for years—or more accurately, I had been kidding Ann—that eventually, one fine day, I would get that dream series job or fall into some other steady gold mine of work that would make all this money madness go away. At this point no one had told me that I had already passed the age barrier in Hollywood where making the big score was a statistical joke. And certainly no one had told Ann-Marie. I was still operating under my twenty-five-year-long delusion that once you joined the club, you had a lifetime membership.

As I kept circling around in the same old delusion, Ann-Marie got mad. Really mad. Inconsolably pissed off. Already in a pretty untenable position before December 10, 1996, she had just been placed in a worse one. She was mad at herself for playing along with my lame Hollywood fantasy for so many frustrating years and not establishing her own beachhead of independence and income. She had been on her own career path as an artist, but had put her work aside to raise the kids, attend to her mother, and take care of the big house. She was mad at the many mutual decisions we had made that were foolhardy and stress-inducing, like overspending, paying private school tuition, and not preparing in any way for the rainiest of days. But mostly she was mad at me. Furious with me. Furious and often condemning.

When I wasn't beating myself up in those dark days, I felt beaten up by her. Paralyzed or not, I had no answer to the hundred questions she posed nightly about our family game plan. My BS about crossing the Hollywood finish line was as convincing as Bill Clinton's definition of "is." After a series of Thursday-night yelling-cum-crying matches (don't ask me why Thursday), we entered this period of prolonged, free-floating estrangement. We were both stuck—I was stuck in a wheelchair, and she was stuck with a guy stuck in a wheelchair. It was messy—life is messy—messier than any fictional account of familial disharmony because it was so relentlessly protracted. In a novel, this kind of long-drawn-out emotional stagnation would bore you to tears. "Get a real job, you moron!" you'd be shouting at around page 150. Or, to either of us, "Stop your incessant bellyaching and get on with your life!"

The living arrangement after I came home almost poetically mirrored the emotional rupture exacerbated by the paralysis.

Ann-Marie lived upstairs; I stayed in my room downstairs. Every night, Ann would go upstairs to the master bedroom, alone, and cry herself to sleep while I would stay downstairs in my cell, alone, and do the same. After a while, I learned to gingerly bump my tail up those stairs, one stair at a time, and we'd be together for a while, away from the other tenants. These weren't exactly romantic get-togethers, but they were a relief from the separation. Then again, the separation was actually the perfect arrangement for the circumstances we were in. It was an ambiguous gray zone between real separation, which neither of us wanted, and a new rapprochement, which was a ways away.

If we had been married three years instead of thirty, or if we had crossed the line of mutual recrimination a few more times, one of us would surely have left the other. Looking back, I think it's a wonder that this didn't happen anyway.

Downstairs, in that room, I felt lonelier than I had felt in the hospital, where at least a nurse would pop in to poke me every fifteen minutes. I needed someone to talk to, to whine to, to write to. It had to be someone who was also wounded, I thought, if not paralyzed, and it most likely had to be a female. I saw this as a matter of conditioning. I was raised by women—my mother, my two older sisters, and a wonderful housekeeper named Gertrude—and like most Oklahoma-bred male Americans, I have had very few soul-baring, tearstained conversations with other males who didn't wear bow ties and weren't raking in $200 an hour.

A lifelong friend of ours living in Eugene, Oregon, Kit Sibert, had lost her husband, the artist and writer Jody Procter, in June 1998. In March of 1998 he developed a hacking cough, and he died of lung cancer three and a half months later. It was a devastating loss. Jody was a brilliant fellow—he had cofounded a conceptual art group, T.R. Uthco, in the 1970s and had worked with another legendary art group of the period, Ant Farm. His real passion, though, was writing. As he was dying, he was working on the final draft of a work of nonfiction, called *Toil*, a beautifully precise depiction of a year in the life of a group of carpenters building a house in Eugene. Jody died without seeing the book reach print. Almost a year to the day later, *Toil*, his only published work, was issued.

I hadn't really confided in anyone besides Ann-Marie for the first year or so of the paralysis; and now, in our upstairs/downstairs separation, she was the one person about whom I needed to confide in someone else. Without planning to, Kit and I began what turned out to be a long, unfettered E-mail correspondence. The great thing about Kit, besides the fact that she has a huge heart and that she too needed someone to confide in, is that she has been a gifted therapist for more than thirty years. She can listen and not judge. Our E-mails were in no way electronic therapy sessions, but Kit brought a forgiving tone that I craved. We developed a bond that seemed to transcend, if not predate, the modern era of professional confiders like therapists, twelve-step programs, and radio call-in shows. We were corresponding by letter, like friends in the nineteenth century, only much faster and without proper punctuation.

Kit got, as the kids would say, "where I was coming from." In her own grief and confusion, she grasped the fact that, in general, I preferred at that point to be alone. Ann-Marie saw this as withdrawal or aloofness, a refusal to face reality and do something practical to deal with our many objective problems. Kit's reply to this, coming a healthy distance away from our accounts payable, was:

> *You certainly have my permission to do nothing. Grief entitles me to do what I need to do to get me through the day and night and sometimes that means unconscious percolating that may look like self-pity or laziness or weakness, but in reality is the profound rumblings of transformation which may mean acceptance or rage or just trying to do the next first thing. . . . You deserve the terrible solitude of grieving that loss of a dream.*

All right! Now you're talking! Apparently I had this solitude coming, and maybe all my unconscious percolating that didn't seem to anyone else to be leading anywhere was in fact leading to a whole new and improved crippled me! To use the AA term I learned from Kit, I could sit on the "pity pot" as long as I wanted. I kept thinking of FDR floating around on a boat in Key West and drinking whiskey for a couple of years. Compared with his withdrawal, mine was like a weekend at the beach.

I could whine to Kit and not feel as though I was whining, just venting. At one point I used the German word "weltschmerz" in an E-mail, and she asked me precisely what it meant. I wrote back that it meant "world sorrow," which is something apparently only Germans do—feel sorry for the whole world. Then there's "schadenfreude," I said, which means "delight at the suffering of others," another fine German invention. And, of course, "angst," which means, ah, angst. And finally, I said, there is the little-known German term "wherinmenschfortuffenscheiss," which means "Why is Allen's life so hard, not that anyone gives a shit?"

Kit was in bad shape, too, of course, stuck in what she called the "grief trenches," so anything she said about herself could also refer to me and anything I said about me referred to her. It got all mixed up. "Some people don't quite realize," she wrote, "what a triumph it is to just get out of bed in the morning. Fucking heroic to not pull the covers back over one's head and sink back all fetal and fucked up." Now, if she had said that to a normal person, they would have thought, Oh, get over it! Husbands die every day. Wah-wah-wah. Get up and do something! My reaction was entirely sympathetic. In fact, I lingered in bed the next morning, feeling gratefully fetal and fucked up.

I had spent my childhood in the presence of a widow—a "professional widow," I once dubbed my mother—so Kit's grief sounded familiar and understandable. She described herself as being like the eyesight-impaired cartoon character Mr. Magoo, "flapping my arms and bumping into reality," and then at night turning into a bat "diving in and out of spiritual caverns." My mother, I now realized more than ever, must have gone through the same brand of torture.

Kit was entirely sympathetic to Ann-Marie as well, which made it slightly easier to deal with Ann's torrents of "black thoughts," as Kit called them. She told me that Ann's rage was probably as old as my guilt about my father and that it would most likely be around for a while. This was hardly good news, but I began to identify Ann's instability with Kit's. They had both lost something important and were stumbling around trying to find an exit. I didn't think, perhaps wrongly, that there was a damn thing I could do in the short term to help either of them. In Ann's case, I favored the non-plan we'd fallen into by default—keep our upstairs/downstairs distance, come together around things like her mother's burgeoning hypochondria or Max's schooling, and just play this thing out.

From my earliest days in the hospital, Ann's plan was to find a new career to ensure some steady income, no matter what happened to me. She immediately went into action, signing up for a fast-track intern teaching program in the Los Angeles Unified School District (LAUSD). This was a program to deal with a severe shortage of teachers by putting qualified "intern" teachers into classrooms and allowing them to simultaneously teach and keep on learning to teach. Ann had taught art but never academic subjects, yet she was not fazed. She was on a mission. She needed the psychological assurance, if not the financial assurance, that she could support the family.

She took a round of college education courses and passed a very difficult statewide test covering everything from early American history to cubic equations, subjects she had never studied before. Within eight months of the onset of my paralysis, she was given her first full-time teaching assignment in the LAUSD: a third-grade class at an entirely Hispanic elementary school near downtown LA. She didn't speak a word of Spanish, but officials told her not to worry—she would have a world of backup. After all, she was new to this. No one would expect her to just walk in and start teaching.

That is, until she arrived for the first day of school.

The class was composed entirely of children who spoke only Spanish. Many of them had serious behavioral and academic problems. They were wild and unruly. Because Ann didn't walk into the room and start ordering them around *en español* like a despotic drill sergeant, they took that as a license to yell, start fights, and ignore her every request. Their lives outside school were often horrifying. A simple exercise in keeping a journal—"How Did You Spend Your Weekend?"—prompted one kid to describe in explicit detail how his uncle had molested him in a public bathhouse. The boy first wrote the episode in Spanish, according to the bilingual policy, and then read it aloud in Spanish. Ann had no idea what was going on until she saw the shock on the face of the bilingual aide.

There was no academic mentor to help Ann, as promised, and there was no established curriculum to guide her lessons. Her only help was the bilingual aide, whose workday was over at noon. The teaching mission was behavioral modification—a perfectly straight military line walking to the lunchroom—not "Reading for Fun." This was no escape from the many crises Ann had to deal with at home. It was just more of the same, in a foreign language.

She came home in tears nightly to a house of loonies who couldn't help themselves, let alone help her. Getting no assistance from the school and put on a battlefield where she had neither the emotional nor pedagogical armor to defend herself, she decided to quit. It was exactly the right thing to do. The other choice was to have a nervous breakdown, and I, for one, thought that one emotional cripple in the family was plenty.

Even if I hadn't been paralyzed and morose and even if

the teaching job hadn't turned out to be insane, Ann still had her aging mother to deal with, a whole other week of Dr. Phil shows. Ann's mother, God bless her soul, was Old Europe transplanted to West LA. She spoke with a thick Swedish accent—"chicken and Jell-O" came out "shicken and yello." She had been born on a farm in southern Sweden in 1909, pre-electricity, and came to America in the early 1930s on a lark. She met and married an equally adventurous Swedish immigrant, Helge Sandberg, in Chicago, and they had a wonderful life together until he passed away in 1973. Since Ann was an only child, her mother lived near us after that until she moved into our big new house in the early 1990s.

Agda was a trip. She was hard-nosed, hardworking, and fiercely independent, insisting on using LA's second-rate public transportation to get around up to a month before her death. She was also fearless. A neighbor once spotted her climbing a ladder into the second floor of our house because she had been locked out; she was eighty-four at the time. She was rarely sick, had zero monetary needs, and seldom demanded attention. Sounds like just the aging mother-in-law every "sandwich-generation" baby boomer would want, right? "Mom's a little feisty, but she's her own gal and we love her for it."

Agda was enormously helpful, especially in seeing to my needs after I came home from the hospital, but at the same time she was enormously intrusive. She planted herself in the central room of the house—the kitchen—and claimed it as her domain. This allowed her to eavesdrop on every private husband/wife and husband/wife/kid conversation within earshot. Since I didn't go upstairs all that often, pretty much every such conversation was at least partially within earshot.

Which meant, given her fading hearing, that she got only part of the information. She would invariably hear through my half-opened door, "I got fired from my new job," instead of what was actually said, "I'm really fired up about my new job."

Agda just added to the pressure, especially in Ann's life. Old people, as everyone over fifty knows full well, are demanding, even the most independent sort. Ann's mother, for instance, was paranoid, especially when it came to her few belongings. She was sure that every housekeeper we employed was stealing from her. This very common old-age fear can be a real hassle when both the supposed perpetrator and the supposed victim are in the same house on the same Monday, every Monday. We went through housekeepers like most people go through a box of detergent. After a while we just gave up.

Plus, as Agda's friends passed away, her social life, not that extensive to begin with, became ever smaller. As a result, she focused more intently on *our* private lives. That would be stressful enough if things were going smoothly. Under the circumstances, it was infuriating. "Did you get hired?" she'd ask every time I came in the door. "Can you pay the mortgage this month?" One of Ann's many tasks was to find diversions for her mother to keep her out of our collective hair.

All these pressures affected and complicated one another, adding up to what seemed like an inescapable morass. One financial solution, for instance, would have been to sell the expensive house. Unfortunately, given the California real estate bust at the time, the house was worth less than our mortgage. If we sold it, we would get no money whatsoever and we'd have to pay taxes on the amount between the actual sale price and the mortgage. In other words, we would have had to pay the government on the money we lost, because the IRS would consider that lost amount a gift from the mortgage company to us. How crazy is that? Also, we had an eighty-six-year-old and an eight-year-old to take care of, along with our upstairs/downstairs separation. We needed the room.

Blaine was twenty and away at school, and his reaction to the family crisis played out far away from any daily encounters with my condition. The possibility that he might drop out and come home never crossed our minds. It's not as if he could plow the fields and feed the hogs while I recuperated. When he first saw me paralyzed, he was knee-deep in finals and had a new girlfriend in tow. This relationship went south not long after, but Blaine contends that the paralysis had nothing to do with it. College life creates its own maelstrom, and it probably distracted Blaine from needlessly worrying about something he could do little to change.

Max seemed to handle this period better than anyone else. For the most part, he later confessed, the whole thing went right by him. He had witnessed the initial attack firsthand; but he was soon told that there was a chance I might walk again, and this news was good enough for him. "I wasn't worried about you," he later said. "I thought everything was going to be OK. I don't think kids take things as hard as adults. They don't understand—you don't think things could possibly go wrong."

The only thing that ever bothered Max was having to explain my paralysis to friends and teachers, "like eight billion times." In fact, after the initial excitement, the only time he even thought about it, he says, was when others would bring it up and react by saying, "Oh, that sucks, man; oh, that really sucks." From Max's eight-year-old vantage point, I was still basically the same guy. He rarely saw me crying or struggling to move, at least in the early days. He'd come to the hospital and later come home, and there I would be, lying in bed, trying to act as normal as possible. When he walked through the door of my room, I'd usually be doing the same things I had always been doing—watching TV, pounding on a laptop, or reading. I had been so sedentary during his first eight years that he didn't see that much of a change. And he didn't want to dwell on the subject of paralysis with either his friends or me, because, in his words, "it dampened the mood a little to talk about it."

Eight years after the fact, I tried to get Max to tell me how he felt about all the tension around the house during the years Mom lived upstairs and I lived down. "What tension?" was basically his reply. "I didn't know it was a dark period. I was just taking it in, going through it. Back then, I wouldn't contemplate; I'd just go. When you're younger, you don't know about life, you just look for the next fun thing that's going to happen to you."

I had always thought Max was embarrassed by my condition and would keep his eight-year-old pals outside if I was out of my prison cell and moving around the house. He now denies feeling like that, and I now think that maybe I was the awkward party. I know I felt a loss of physical contact with Max that he never felt as strongly. Though it may sound like the most cloying of TV-movie clichés, one of the things I missed most was playing sports with him. I had spent countless hours throwing a baseball around with Blaine when he was ten, and looked forward to the same mindless athletic amusement with Max. When Blaine first heard that I was paralyzed, the images that immediately came to his mind were "crystal-clear memories of my dad, the athlete." He remembered playing catch in the middle of the street until we ran out of sunlight, my mid-eighties jogging infatuation, my red eighties Nike running shoes, and my coaching his T-ball games. For Max, my love of physical activity was little more than old family yarns.

Within a very short period after the paralysis, I couldn't throw a baseball or a football ten feet. I couldn't raise my arm above my head without excruciating pain. The overuse of my shoulders in wheeling around in the chair soon caused enough osteoarthritis to cancel out my throwing motion. I couldn't challenge Max in basketball or teach him how to hit a golf ball or lay down a bunt. As it turned out, Max quickly got so good at basketball that I couldn't have challenged him anyway. He never liked baseball, and his interest in golf lasted about a week. Still, this was one small, seemingly inconsequential area of life that really brought my impairment home.

Agda Sandberg died in January 1999, just short of her ninetieth birthday. Her passing, sad as it was, freed us to begin to envision a different future. She was never the source of any of our real problems, only a minute-to-minute witness. And in her passing not only did we see ourselves differently; we could again see her, apart from our own worries, as the spirited and caring person she always was.

Soon after her death, Max had his own crisis, which, ironically, became his way of seeing my paralysis in perspective. On a school camping trip in the Sierras, he witnessed the drowning of one of his ten-year-old school friends. Max was in the swimming pond at the same time and remembers his friend pulling on his shirtsleeve to keep from going under. Thinking he was joking, Max swam away, as did several other kids, until someone finally noticed that the victim was no longer visible. "It was freezing as hell out there, the sun was setting, and I remember standing there with Nehemiah [a friend] saying, 'Oh, crap, what's happening?' and Nehemiah was shivering. . . ."

This remains a painful memory for Max, a memory about death that is intertwined in his mind with my ongoing paralysis and his grandmother's death only weeks before. It was his breaking point, his moment to experience something deep and disturbing and learn to transcend it. Not long after, our three-month-old puppy, Darla, swallowed a quarter and two pennies and was close to dying from metal poisoning. In the scheme of things, it doesn't seem like much, but to a ten-year-old, and to his parents, her recovery was a joyous event. In Max's view, that was the beginning of the end of the dark period.

One marital issue that wasn't all that big an issue was sex. "We have our ways." That's how the spouse of one well-known paralytic explained their post-paralysis sex life to some nosy reporter. It's the perfect answer, at once ambiguous and titillating. It could mean, "We do things now that you only dream of your wife or husband doing, and it's freaking mind-blowing." Or it could mean, "We sit around, eat chocolate, and read each other passages from Anaïs Nin's *Delta of Venus*." Or, if you read this in a small-town newspaper in Kansas, it probably means that Blanche and Ned found a fun hobby to do together like collecting redwood burl tables or raising shi tzus.

Well, we have "our ways" too, and they are nothing like the ways we had before the paralysis. First of all, they don't involve the use of any of my, ah, equipment, since my equipment is in a long-term state of hibernation. After seeing one too many "when it's the right time" erectile dysfunction commercials, I looked into the possibility that there was some biochemical help out there for me. My urologist explained all the options. Actually, there was one main option, called injection therapy. You inject a drug, prostaglandin, into the penis, which then becomes engorged and ready for action. There are pumping devices you can have implanted for this purpose, too, but I wasn't interested. Unfortunately, even injection could not provide any sensation (that is, pleasure), movement, or relief. My engorged friend would function more or less like an inanimate marital device that happened to be attached to my body. From a scientific view, this may be appealing; but from the practical point of view of either participating spouse, it sucked.

Nevertheless, we have our ways, which you can flesh out in any libidinous fashion you wish. "Do you think they ... ?" "Oh, no, they only do that in France." In addition to those ways, we stumbled across something else that may even be more profound, and more deeply satisfying, than physical sex. I know many of you are shaking your heads in violent opposition to this line of thought, but, setting your dreams of four-hour erections aside, there is something that happens to a long-term, loving connubial relationship when one or the other partner becomes permanently impaired.

Assuming you survive the dark years—or maybe, in your case, only the dark weeks—things tend to get more passionate, way more passionate, in the "ardent" meaning of the word "passion," not the *Desperate Housewives* meaning. The dictionary defines "ardent" as "having or expressing great depth of feeling." This is different from "having or expressing great depth of animal lust." You feel more. You spend a lot more time feeling genuinely in love. Your heart actually swells. This is not just something that happens when a cartoon Prince Charming spots a cartoon Sleeping Beauty of the same animal species and his cartoon heart leaps out of his chest, becomes twice as big as his head, and pounds like a tom-tom. Your heart stays in your chest, but it feels heavier. You look at your spouse at least three times a day and say, "Boy, am I glad I married you."

Recognizing such renewed passion was still a ways off for both Ann and me. But even in our prolonged upstairs/downstairs estrangement, it may have been the stuff beneath the anger, guilt, and disappointment that kept us going. Not that we had any place to go just yet. We had more hand-wringing, soul-searching, and desperation to experience. We were still middle-aged adolescents.

EIGHT

FAITH, WILL, AND DR. STRANGELOVE

THE SEEMINGLY ENDLESS BOUT OF emotional paralysis persisted for at least another year after Ann's mother's death, leaving plenty of downtime for rudderless mental percolating, conscious and unconscious. Between writer-for-hire jobs, none of which was particularly challenging or career-cranking, I spent a lot of time thinking about crippled role models. Christopher Reeve was an obvious choice, but he turned his condition into his life's work, and I had no urge to do that. That was an assignment for Clark Kent. I was more of the Jimmy Olsen type.

The quintessential paralytic who first occurred to me took me back to college: Sir Clifford Chatterley, cuckold husband of arguably the randiest woman in the history of fiction, Lady Constance Chatterley. This may be a little esoteric for some, but all English majors and lovers of dirty literary masterpieces will know what I'm talking about. D. H. Lawrence's *Lady Chatterley's Lover*, privately printed in 1928, is about a rich woman who has raucous sexual trysts with Oliver Mellors, the gamekeeper on her husband's English estate. They go into his little woodsman's hut every chance they get and make liberating, orgiastic love. Meanwhile, the poor husband, Sir Clifford, is back at the big house with his nurse and nanny, Mrs. Bolton, writing stories and licking his psychic wounds. Permanently paralyzed while fighting in the Great War—World War I—Clifford Chatterley never leaves his wheelchair.

Sir Clifford can't make love to his wife, because he is a eunuch. He is hors de combat, as he politely puts it, meaning "out of action, disabled." He's not a bad sort for a rich English guy, but he has lost all passion for life—he is emotionally distant, distracted, cut off. In Lawrence's words, "He tended to become vague, absent, and to fall into fits of vacant depression." He now lives only in his head, and this drives Lady C. nuts. By page 27 of the unexpurgated version, she is having her way with a male guest on the third floor while her husband is alone with his thoughts on the first floor. (Please note the upstairs/downstairs arrangement. Maybe I should have put a surveillance camera up there.)

When I first read this novel in a college lit class, I had nothing but disdain for this pathetic Sir Invalid as he puttered around in his pathetic gas-driven wheelchair, which he couldn't get up a hill without Mellors's help. As a writer, Sir Clifford has his stories and his quest for "the bitch goddess

Success," but he thinks of humanity as something to observe and inspect from a distance—in Lawrence's terms, "like a man looking down a microscope, or up a telescope." Chatterley is aging fast, helpless, and so screwed up that he encourages his wife to have sex with any old bloke just to bear him an heir. Reading this at age nineteen, I cheered her escape into the lustful arms of her working-class paramour.

Thirty-some years later, I suddenly realized, I'm a hell of a lot closer to Clifford Chatterley than to the studly gamekeeper. I'm confined to a wheelchair and I stay indoors a lot. I live in my head and prefer to be alone. I'm emotionally absent for days on end and often fall into "fits of vacant depression." Some critics think that Lawrence was describing himself in this character—Lawrence's own wife apparently shacked up with an Italian peasant—but in any case, he got the forlorn paralytic down cold. Reading the story again, I now *liked* Sir Clifford. He was the one character grounded in a reality I knew. He was my kind of guy: moody, self-absorbed, and absolutely no fun to be around.

His fate, unfortunately, was awful. Would my wife finally run off with an earthy gardener or maybe the UPS guy? Would I then spend the rest of my sorry life with a ballbuster nurse like Mrs. Bolton?

So, figuring that this was a dated view of the disabled, I looked around for more uplifting fictional models. Until a few years ago, I soon discovered, the paralyzed were not given the best parts. As far as my decidedly slapdash research took me, the three most prevalent disabled personality types were: Pathetic, Mean, or Crazy. Clifford Chatterley is certainly the pathetic type. For another example, think of Tiny Tim in Dickens's *A Christmas Carol*. Tim is not the typical Dickens waif who defies adult authority and runs around London knocking off top hats. He's a sweet little crippled boy with a homemade crutch who melts the heart of a heartless old geezer. He's one of Jerry's kids. You'll never see him lashing out at an unfair world. If he survived at all, he probably grew up to take his dad's bean-counting job down at Scrooge's version of Ditec.com. We love the spunky little guy and pity him at the same time.

My favorite Mean Crippled in the movies is Mr. Potter, the greedy banker in *It's a Wonderful Life*. Why is the archvillain in this beloved, tearstained American classic in a wheelchair? The actor Lionel Barrymore was already in a wheelchair, but in this role it made him more villainous, that's why. He's grouchy all day because he's wheelchair-bound, or maybe vice versa. No way is this old coot going to put up with any "sentimental hogwash" from liberal do-gooders like Jimmy Stewart. Imperiously wheeling around in his chair, snuggled in his lap blanket, bitter, cantankerous, and relentlessly avaricious, someone all handicapped-Americans can admire.

Among the crazy and impaired, you can't beat Dr. Strangelove, the immortal warmonger in the power chair played by Peter Sellers in the movie of the same name. A first-ballot shoo-in for the Paralyzed Hall of Fame, Strangelove is a psychotic pervert, and paralysis has everything to do with his insanity. Only a deformed fascist like him could embrace death with such gusto. His mechanical "heil Hitler" salute is in perfect sync with his mechanical explanations of global destruction and human suffering. When it's clear that the world is about to be wiped out, Dr. Strangelove is so excited, so perversely aroused, that he stands up and walks like Frankenstein. "Mein Führer," he bellows, "I can walk!"

Strangelove, of course, is a joke. He is both a parody of Henry Kissinger/Wernher von Braun Teutonic types and of all the mad movie villains in wheelchairs. The character takes the mean, life-hating, death-obsessed, impotent, degenerate cripple to its logical conclusion. Unlike mean old Mr. Potter, Strangelove doesn't want to destroy the Building and Loan. He wants to destroy the whole world.

If I imitated these losers, I'd have nothing but bitterness and misanthropy in my future. I too was hors de combat and depressed about it. I kept looking for something a little more upbeat to hang my hat on. I was a big fan of the Jimmy Stewart character in Hitchcock's *Rear Window*, a true hero stuck in a wheelchair, but he was only temporarily non-ambulatory; his broken legs would heal, and he would have no trouble in the bedding-down department with Grace Kelly.

By the mid-1960s, things began to change, at least in the movies. The Vietnam war, unfortunately, created a lot of wheelchair users and a new spirit of disabled defiance arose. No more Tiny Tims with their little hands out for a morsel of fruitcake from Mr. Scrooge. Now, refreshingly, you had the Jon Voight character in *Coming Home*. I'm sure there were many admirable, or at least understandable, disabled types in films before this—see *The Best Years of Our Lives* (1946) or Marlon Brando's film *The Men* (1950)—but Jon Voight, in the age of the living room war, was as real as the wounded vets on the evening news. He was nasty and withdrawn, then came back to life on-screen. And he got the girl! The crippled guy got the girl, and Jane Fonda, no less.

This was more like it, I thought. Vietnam also produced a real-life paraplegic, Ron Kovic, played by Tom Cruise in the movie *Born on the Fourth of July*. In a much-touted performance in a much-touted film, Cruise marched the character through the often excruciating stages of guilt, pain, self-hatred, and dissolution until Kovic triumphed as a leader of Vietnam Veterans Against the War. You couldn't help feeling respectful, even if you supported the war. Only a few wars before, Clifford Chatterley came home a ball-less cynic. Ron Kovic rolled right onto the floor of the 1972 Republican Convention and shook his fist at Richard Nixon.

I'm no Leonard Maltin of *Le Cinema du Crip*, but one other post-sixties film about paralysis deserves mention, considered by many in the disabled community to be the best cinematic depiction of the condition ever done—Neal Jimenez's *Waterdance*. This film, starring Eric Stoltz and Wesley Snipes, focuses on a trio of young, newly paralyzed men much closer to the norm than I am. They meet each other in a ward at a rehab hospital and must not only deal with their own demons but also do battle with one another's bad sides. There are no happy endings here, no glorious denouement of redemption and transcendence. In fact, the leading character, played by Stoltz, tells his devoted girlfriend, played by Helen Hunt, to go back to her husband. The whole film is a sobering acknowledgment that most people with paralysis do not become beacons of inspiration on *Oprah*. They just muddle through.

There's one absurd scene in *Waterdance* that I'll never forget. One night, out of nowhere, a troupe of spirited suburban square dancers comes bounding into the rehab ward to raise the roof. It's a frightening spectacle of string ties and gingham skirts—lanky tire salesmen and their chub-a-kins wives—and the last thing that would cheer up a paralytic. The do-si-doers don't get it, of course. Like many people, they fail to see the line between encouragement and insult.

Nevertheless, paralytic inspiration now abounds: Tom Cruise's portrayal of Ron Kovic; Christopher Reeve; unrepentant porno don Larry Flynt with his solid-gold wheelchair; ex-Senator Max Cleland, a triple amputee; Joe Hartzler, the prosecutor with MS who nailed Timothy McVeigh; and a hundred other public disabled people, real and fictional. The public image of disability has changed radically, and the pendulum has swung way off in the other direction. These disabled people, at least on the surface, are so energetic, so strong-willed, and often so selflessly dedicated to social change and personal achievement that they put a lot of pressure on the Jimmy Olsens like me to climb the highest mountain and blaze a trail to world peace. *Waterdance* aside, there is almost no such thing in the media as an average, workaday, beer-drinking guy in a chair anymore, if there ever was. There are no paralyzed Ralph Kramdens or George Costanzas. Occasionally, a "normal" wheelchair user shows up on TV but not very often. You've got to run (or roll) a marathon, sadistically mow down another wheelchair gladiator in Death Match Rugby, or stop a war to get any ink these days.

If I ever had a public role model, it was Franklin Roosevelt. What appealed to me from early on in my impaired state were not his accomplishments or his politics. It was his style. I loved his public act: never show anyone that you are impaired. Never let anyone see you struggle or sweat. Don't talk about your disability or let others talk about it. Don't use it to win sympathy or sympathy votes, and never put yourself in the position of becoming the poster boy for "Triumph over Paralysis."

What he seemed to be saying by his public performance was simple: what does being paralyzed have to do with anything?

This kind of blithe stoicism seems odd by today's standards of public soul-baring. Nowadays, the least complication or setback in life seems to open the floodgates of self-examination, therapy, spiritual conversion, and public witnessing. Daytime talk shows investigate ad nauseam issues that were once taboo, such as why a housewife has a messy pantry or why her husband spends hours web-surfing plumprumps.com. This confessional impulse can become a problem when you have something to confess, like what it's really like to live this way. You don't want to "overtalk it," as Blaine once accused me of doing. On the other hand, if FDR had left a memoir of paralysis, he could have inspired or at least informed millions. It's often hard to know where to draw the line between self-exposure and self-restraint. Roosevelt at least reminds us that we don't have to talk about a disability at every turn. It's not a requirement of being paralyzed.

Evidently, there are perhaps eleven seconds of film of FDR in leg braces. His deftness at never being photographed in a situation that would reveal his disability was a political necessity at the time. It also depended on a widespread media conspiracy. Today, with our scandal-addicted press corps watching, campaigning for president from a chair would be tough sledding. Truth be told, few bald men in my lifetime have been elected president, let alone someone who couldn't stand tall on an aircraft carrier, slap a few backs, and act like a commander in chief. Paralysis is, after all, a deformity and, as I mentioned earlier, often connotes weakness or ill health. Bob Dole ran for president with one bad arm, and though he lost, at least no one blamed the arm. But a president in a wheelchair? My guess is that this candidate, man or woman, has to get in line behind an ambulatory female president, an African-American president, a Hispanic president, a Jewish president, and maybe a president born in Austria. But who knows? Only a few years back wheelchair users didn't have access to public toilets. Things change.

What do you do when you're stuck in a foxhole under heavy fire? Prayer is one option, or so the company chaplain recommends. Some soldiers just start shooting like madmen (option two); some give up, curl up, and wait to die or be captured (option three). And some choose option four, the practical approach—get the hell out of there tout de suite.

After I became paralyzed, I chose a combination of options one and four and began to pray a lot. I prayed for recovery, for strength, for solace. I prayed for any kind of inspiration I could find. In the hospital, I prayed on the hour, usually after a spontaneous crying jag. For a while, I was a fifteen-to-twenty-prayers-a-day man, about the same number of Pall Malls I used to smoke a day when I was a smoker. And others prayed for me. A dear friend, Jodi Sibert, called a long list of people to create a prayer circle on my behalf. The idea was that at a certain time—say, Sunday morning at eleven o'clock—everyone in the circle would ask their higher power to help me survive and bounce back. I was extremely touched by this gesture. It was a collective outpouring of good feeling.

People began to send me inspirational books that they thought would help me to "grow," "heal," or find the "true source" of life. Most of these books were later sold at a garage sale, unread. A close friend, Ted Steinberg, told a friend of his, a born-again Texan named Billy Bob Harris, about my plight, and Billy Bob got right on my case with the Almighty. Billy Bob is larger than life, a small-town country boy who became a celebrity Dallas stockbroker, went to jail as part of an insider-trading debacle, and came out full of the gospel. I knew Billy Bob through Ted and liked him a lot, so when he started calling me to tell me that faith would help me through this, I didn't feel that I was getting either shucked or jived. His faith didn't strike me as a political pose or psychological bullying. He wasn't trying to turn my head around on the issue of gay marriage or intelligent design. He was just trying to help.

Billy Bob sent me a book, *Power Through Constructive Thinking*, by Emmett Fox, a Christian motivational writer and speaker who had died in 1951. Fox had some relationship to the "new thought" movement of the early twentieth century—a movement that William James defined as the "religion of healthy-mindedness"—and also had some influence over the founders of AA. I didn't know anything about Fox, and I'm still not quite sure what "new thought" is, but I read the book because Billy Bob thought I should. If it didn't quite change my life, it made me feel much better about myself.

"This book shows that your destiny is really in your own hands," Mr. Fox asserts up-front, "because it is impossible to think one thing and produce another.... It shows that fear is the ultimate cause or Tap-Root of all sickness, failure, and disappointment. And it shows the only possible method of overcoming fear."

I don't want to wander astray into a short course on this take-matters-into-your-own-hands theology, but it struck me that Mr. Fox's method was really more a state of mind than a religious practice. His version of this state of mind recognized the presence of a supreme power in the practical solution of human problems. My own version of the idea was a state of mind characterized by certainty—victory over doubt as a mental process. What I heard in his sermonizing was the tone of voice I had heard from my midwestern grandparents, probably passed on by their midwestern grandparents: the unshakable conviction that there is a solution to every problem—and, by God, just alter your thinking and you will find salvation, without a doubt.

And what about doubt? "There are many who appreciate the power of faith, but lament that they do not possess it, and fear that because of this they can make no progress in Truth. There is no such need for such apprehension.... As long as your heart is really clear of ill-will, you are perfectly safe."

Get it? Think positively. What could be more American than that? Keep your heart clear of ill will and question all thoughts of failure, disappointment, jealousy, or self-condemnation. In search of this healthy-mindedness, Mr. Fox counseled, figure it out yourself. "When your usual methods of treating a problem do not seem to be bringing results, it is a good plan to discontinue them altogether for a time, and to work exclusively for inspiration instead."

So endeth the lesson.

I could take only so much positive thinking at this point, so I generally forgot about seeking divine guidance and got back to feeling sorry for myself. But the subject of faith kept popping up—it's always in the air, at least in America. Kit Sibert argued that whether or not God was a fiction, He or She or It worked—even if It worked only because the believer thought It worked, like a spiritual placebo, in the same way that the Cowardly Lion found courage as he sought out the Wizard of Oz to give him courage. And if I didn't see this, maybe that was because I was looking in the wrong place. By example, she told me an old AA chestnut, "The Eskimo Story":

> A drunk in a bar regales a crowd about once getting stranded in barren Alaska. His sled dog dies and the man begins to freeze to death. He prays to God that if God saves him, he will stop drinking forever. Another guy at the bar is puzzled—"But you're alive and you're still drinking." The drunk replies, "Hell, God didn't do anything. Some Eskimo came by and saved me."

I got the point, but it didn't change my attitude. In the end, I just threw in the towel. I couldn't muster up the faith to use a spiritual mind-set to direct my actions. I decided to drop the subject—not close the door, dogmatically, but not open it, either. Keep the matter ambiguous, open to further consideration, should that occur. Bob Dole was once asked in an interview on television if he believed there was life after death. His answer: "I don't know." That, I decided, was a perfectly good answer to the vagaries of spiritual redemption in general.

The psychology at work went something like this. In my relatively helpless condition, I felt that pleading for divine intervention—asking others for help—was something I had been doing ever since my father slipped on the ice and died. At this juncture such pleading made me feel impotent, small, and even a little bit silly. The resolve and equanimity I was looking for, I slowly came to realize, were not a favor I asked of the universe, but an internal reordering that only I had authority over. In my particular foxhole, in a mostly unconscious coming to terms, I had to willfully manufacture the belief that I could get through this. And to do that, I had to posit that I was in it alone.

So, at this point, I had worked my way through Clifford Chatterley, Mr. Potter, Jon Voight, FDR, and the religion of healthy-mindedness. Only in retrospect did I realize that my only real role model was my late mother, Laura Emma Allen Rucker. The Fifth Commandment says: "Honor thy father and mother." I never much honored my mother by doing what she wanted me to do during her lifetime; but as she was dying I realized that I had honored her by becoming like her, at least in the way I dealt with life after paralysis.

There are a lot of books out now honoring the parents of baby boomers, "The Greatest Generation," and their courage, sacrifice, and good sense. If I wrote a book-length tribute to my mother, it would not be an eye-moistening hagiography. She was a loving parent, but she was not all that easy to hang out with, at least for me. She had a faster mind and a thinner waist than anyone else in the room, and she often had such a critical edge to her voice that the simple question "How's the weather?" could set you back on your heels. "Gee, Mother, I think it's a little chilly. . . ." "Oh, it's not chilly at all. You are such a namby-pamby, Allen. Is that why you wouldn't go fight in Vietnam, because you might catch a cold?" She was, in a word, imperious, and her domineering manner was hard for a lot of people, including some of her own kids, to handle.

With a stony look or a biting retort, she could make you feel like a useless, lamebrained troll.

My mother was a taskmaster. She wanted her four children to excel, to make her proud, all the more so because they had no father to back them up. She had one life plan, it seemed—raise four children she could read about in the newspaper—and part of that plan was to complete this task on her own. She had a little wrought-iron tchotchke that sat on the windowsill over the kitchen sink during my entire childhood. It was some kind of chicken in a defiant pose—maybe the "little red hen" of lore—and the legend read, defiantly, "I'll do it myself." For all intents and purposes, that was her lifelong mantra.

She often spoke in adages, all in the direction of buck up and get on with the task. "I pitied the man who had no shoes until I saw a man who had no feet." "This too shall pass." "When I was a child, I spake as a child . . . but when I became a man, I put away childish things." Many of these sayings had biblical intonations, picked up from a lifetime of Methodist study classes. She was a churchgoer, but she never promoted selflessness or devotion as the path to righteousness. She promoted self-starting. "Sell yourself," she must have said 10,000 times. Get off the mat and sell yourself.

She got this can-do ethos from her own father, Dr. Clinton M. Allen, a Kansas farm boy who rode a horse in the Oklahoma land rush of 1893 and later earned a PhD in psychology from Columbia University. Clinton Allen had a brother who signed his name with an X, but my grandfather wrote books on intelligence testing. His sense of the possible rubbed off on all three of his daughters, and especially on the middle one, Laura.

My mother had lived briefly in New York as a very young girl while her father was earning his doctorate, and she yearned for a life of urban style and grace. She was always throwing around references to "the Waldorf" or "oysters Rockefeller" as if she belonged in that world, not in small-town Oklahoma. She couldn't afford to buy a mansion in East Egg like the character Jay Gatsby in *The Great Gatsby*, but she had Gatsby's hunger to be something that she wasn't.

So she faked it. She drove hand-me-down Cadillacs from her brother-in-law in Tulsa; maintained a big, showy house; paid her monthly dues at a country club though she neither played golf nor swam; kept her weight at a trim 101 pounds, and perfected the air of an astute, sharp-tongued woman of leisure. This conflicted somewhat with the reality that she had no money, no career, and four kids to shepherd from Tri-Hi-Y to piano lessons and back. Put it this way: she was always the best-dressed woman at the local cafeteria on Tuesday nights. She took workaday jobs and sold soft drinks at the Little League games, but in her mind she was always Mrs. Ralph Rucker, wife of the prominent physician Dr. Ralph Rucker, though Dr. Ralph Rucker had been dead for twenty or thirty years.

I fought with my mother constantly—she called me a coward to my face for not going to Vietnam—and I spent my adult life a good 1,500 to 2,000 miles away from her spurious judgments and critical assaults. She was easier to love that way. When she was in her seventies, Ann-Marie and I took her on a cross-country trip to visit the Grand Canyon and other points in the southwest and she spent the entire journey criticizing Blaine, then eleven, for his "atrocious" table manners. One night in Santa Fe, she got uncharacteristically tipsy—she hated to lose control—and confessed that at age nineteen she had wanted to be a dancer, but her stern Calvinist father put the kibosh on that dream. Something seemed to put the kibosh on every dream she ever had for herself.

But, but, but ... she had ferocious resolve, an unshakable conviction in her own view of the world, however skewed, and she was fearless. She had that Emmett Fox certainty of purpose. There are a thousand ways she could have been brought down by circumstances—a bad second or third marriage, financial ruin, alcoholism (very popular in the 1950s in small-town Oklahoma), or just resigning herself to a tawdry second-class life. But she persevered. With the fortitude of a martyr, she took the hardest route possible—alone—and pulled it off, at considerable cost to her personal happiness. She was a narcissist who spent a good part of her best years helping others, including me, succeed. That was the hand she was dealt, and she played it like Amarillo Slim.

I wouldn't have claimed any of my mother's qualities—will, conviction, fearlessness—before or after I became paralyzed. I always saw myself, at least in my worst moments, as relatively will-challenged, of malleable conviction, and often fearful. The fact that I didn't fall apart in the face of this crisis still amazes me, and I give most of the credit to my mother's example. She was my measure of how to act in an awful situation. I had no ideology, religious or political, to bolster me; no metaphysical backstop; no grand mission to propel me forward. I yearned for one or the other, but nothing came to mind. My only mission was to persevere, take care of my family, and get back to work. At the lowest point of my so-called recovery, I didn't have a clue as to how to do that. I only had, thanks to my mother, a gut sense that I would eventually figure it out.

Maybe there is a gene for perseverance that I inherited from my raised-four-kids-by-herself mother, passed along by her overachieving father. Why are some people able to cope with adversity while others fall apart? The whole thing could just be a roll of the genetic dice and have little or nothing to do with role models, personal character, or rules of living. Never underestimate your genes. After all, they are the only ones you've got.

My mother died at ninety-two; and for most of her last years, she was physically healthier than most of her children. She outlived one daughter—my sister Rosalind—and all of her own siblings. Mother's mind started slipping a few years before her death. Eventually, every time I talked to her, I had to announce again that I was paralyzed. "Paralyzed!," she'd respond in a huff. "Paralyzed! Why doesn't anyone tell *me* these things?" Self-centered to the end.

Nature, nurture, or luck, it was a weird twist of fate that the person I was most intimidated by as a child and distanced myself from as an adult became the person I sought to emulate when the Big Test was slipped under the door. And by the time I realized this, sadly, she was too far gone to hear my thanks.

Honor your father and mother, indeed. One day, in ways you can't imagine, they could save your life.

NINE

THE UPSIDE
OF INFIRMITY

AND THEN IT WAS OVER.

Next.

Almost imperceptibly, the black mood that had lingered for years slowly abated. However it happened, it happened. The two-year emotional downturn that began around the time the doctor at UCLA told me I'd never walk again began to subside around the dawn of 2000. Maybe it had some-thing to do with all the hubbub and how-to-set-your-clock confusion around the new millennium. I'll never know. With questionable help from all my own mental gymnastics, mood swings, and declarations of this or that tenet of existence, the grief, inertia, and self-pity mysteriously worked their way through my system. They came; they dug in for a long stay; then they left. There was no sudden flash of light, no second-act reversal or third-act climax like you might learn in a master screenwriting course. The dark cloud just left.

As I realized that something had fundamentally changed, I thought of a short story by Raymond Carver called "Fever." It's about a high school teacher whose wife runs off to Hollywood with the drama and glassblowing teacher "to do something with her talent," leaving him with two small children. He is in an understandable state of confusion, anger, and humiliation. She then steps in, long distance from LA, to help him out, offering him sympathy (oddly) and finding a take-charge country woman to be the nanny and run his domestic life.

Things are going great until one day he develops a fever. His estranged wife counsels him, "Remember, sickness is a message about your health and well-being. It's telling you things. Keep a record." In the midst of the fever, the nanny announces that she is relocating with her husband to a mink ranch in Oregon. This prompts the teacher to pour out his heart to her for the first and only time, and to express his profound sadness at his wife's betrayal. As he talks, suddenly the fever begins to dissipate. As the nanny drives away, the man knows that "something important had been settled" and he can go on with his life.

I knew things were different one night during an episode of *Law & Order*. The story was about a woman who wanted to exercise her right to die because she was a hopeless paralytic. "I'm weak," she said, "tired, in constant pain, incontinent, and I'll have to spend the rest of my life in a wheelchair!"

My response was, "So? What's the problem?"

Of course, nothing objective had changed. In fact, on the surface, things looked worse than ever. Ann-Marie was through with full-time teaching but had gone back to work as a substitute teacher, and it was often a grind. I was flying off to Orlando to write Disney World parade shows, and I had just come off a major disappointment involving a pilot research project at UCLA on spinal cord rehabilitation. The big idea of the project was that the spinal cord was smart—capable of recognizing and retaining neural patterns—and could be taught the neural process of walking without direct input from the brain. Through repetitive motion, the lower spine could figure out walking in the same way that a baby, falling on its bum a thousand times, figures it out. I couldn't wait to sign up. I wanted that degree from the University of Small Steps.

I tried to enroll in the project but was cruelly and summarily rejected as a paralyzed guinea pig. Given the size and placement of my nerve damage, apparently my spine wasn't going to learn squat. Plus, even if the experiment proved to be the breakthrough of the ages, I wouldn't benefit a lick.

I continued to underestimate my condition, get periodically ill, and land back in the hospital too many times. The main problems were fever and infections from wounds, the millstone of paralysis. Some ulcers simply wouldn't heal at all and needed skin grafts—that is, more surgery. It was about this time that I discovered Dr. Ralph Potkin and hyperbaric oxygen therapy. Except for my brief encounter with Ram Dass, this lengthy stay in a glassed-in coffin was medically beneficial but a colossal waste of time. I kept a regular daily appointment to lie on my back and do nothing. I've often thought that this protracted time-out—two hours a day for six months—may have had as much to do with the emotional shift that soon followed as any grand insight on my part. Maybe the synapses of acceptance were stimulated by all that pressurized oxygen to the brain. Franklin Roosevelt floated around in a boat in the Keys, drinking whiskey and telling jokes. I reclined like a mummy in a vacuum-packed space capsule watching reruns on television and listening to banal pop-rock ditties like "Don't Stop Believin'." I would have kept doing it for another six months, but the wounds healed and the Writers Guild Health Fund stopped paying for my oxy-o-therapy.

Lying in that airtight cocoon day in and day out, I had plenty of time to ponder the other side of the paralysis coin, the "sunny side." This kind of all-American, Norman Vincent Peale–styled positive thinking seemed to be what I needed. I was a little tired of hearing the standard chin-up bromides: "When one door closes, another opens." "What doesn't kill us makes us stronger." I needed bromides that would attack the specific issue of paralysis and would make it seem survivable or even benign. I pictured a daily flip calendar with a spirit-lifting benefit on each page. (When I ran out of benefits, I'd fill in the rest of the days with birds of North America.) For example:

February 13. YOU'LL NEVER AGAIN HEAR THE WORDS "HEY, WHILE YOU'RE UP, COULD YOU GET ME . . ."

You're never "up"! The rest of the world is always up and will automatically ask you if you want another bagel, a gin and tonic, or a second helping of baked ziti. If you play your cards right, this extends to every petty urge you'll ever have. Drop a sly reference to your high regard for Peter O'Toole, and someone in the room will plead, "Oh, please, let me drive to the Valley and pick up that special-edition DVD of *Lawrence of Arabia*. No prob. I'll be back in three hours." This urge to please you will wear off soon enough, so start your wish list now.

March 15. YOU'LL NEVER AGAIN SEE YOURSELF NUDE IN A FULL-LENGTH MIRROR.

Nor will you have to suck in your gut every time you stand up. Nor will you pop the middle button on your favorite suit coat after a trip to the Olive Garden. It's a whole shift in your body image. Put on twenty pounds, and people will say, "You look so good! You're not sallow or emaciated or anything!" You still have to stay healthy, of course, and learn to deal with the fact that no member of the opposite sex, no matter what age, will ever see you the same way again. This is not easy. Unless you are twenty, are built like a linebacker, and enjoy displaying your *cojones* by surfing in a wheelchair, no woman will ever wink at you again. Especially if you are over fifty and tend to nod off at parties.

June 22. YOU'LL NEVER BE "MRS." ANYONE IN PRISON.

If you're thinking about robbing a bank, hang your hat on this good news: when you are incarcerated, you will not have to fight off the advances of your love-starved cellmate named "The Jackhammer." You are no more attractive to him than you are to the good-looking checkout girl at the AM/PM. He'll probably see you as the therapist he never had and spend nights telling you about the boyhood sled his father pitched into the fireplace.

June 29. YOU'LL NEVER HAVE TO "STAND UP" FOR YOURSELF AGAIN.

In prison or out, you'll never have to defend your honor, because you can't defend your honor. You can't "step outside" and go a couple of rounds in the parking lot. You can tongue-lash the biggest, meanest guy in the joint or the driver of the Dodge Dakota who just cut you off on the freeway, and what is he going to do? Punch out a crippled guy? It's never happened in the history of fisticuffs.

August 17. YOU HAVE TO BUY A NEW PAIR OF SHOES ONLY ONCE EVERY FIVE YEARS.

You can't beat the savings. Your shoes never touch the ground, thus never wear out. Also, they cease being a fashion statement. You can wear furry little house slippers with an Armani suit and no one will snicker or point. But why waste money on an Armani suit? The Men's Wearhouse, or even Foot Locker, will do just fine. No one cares. You'll never have to tuck in another shirt or wear a tie, a belt, a suit coat, or anything else that might further constrict your already constricted movement. So be comfortable and wear a purple velour sweat suit to your cousin's wedding. People will just think you are "eccentric," poor dear.

September 26. THERE IS NO TASK SO SMALL THAT YOU CAN'T SIDESTEP IT WITH YOUR HEAD HELD HIGH.

When it's fall and the gutters are full of leaves, no one will be handing you a ladder and rake. You'll never be asked to move a piano, carry in the groceries, wash the car, paint the hallway, or empty the trash. Did you ever try to mop a floor in a wheelchair? You keep wheeling over the wet area or getting the mop tentacles stuck in your wheels. You can still do the dishes and fold laundry, but that's about the time you feel you need to lie down for a minute. Crossword puzzles quickly become your main area of household expertise.

October 1. THIS IS YOUR LUCKY DAY! (IF YOU'RE MALE, ANYWAY.)

Why? Because today a beautiful woman could see you across a crowded room, wave, run over, and bend down to kiss you, as women almost always do. When this happens, you'll get to admire her breasts from about three inches away! And she won't care because she doesn't think of you as a sexual anything. Man, are you lucky!

I could go on and on with these flip pages of found fortune. For the wheelchair user, for instance, baseball tickets are usually half price, the designated seating is usually close to the beer stand, and your buddy will insist on bringing you the beer and nachos. Besides free parking, you get free full service at the gas station and enthusiastic bag-hauling service at the supermarket. Or consider this: if you have a big butt, no one will ever again call you "Big Butt." When it's leg-wrestling time after dinner, you can't lose, because you can't play. And if it's arm-wrestling time, people will let you win! The full list is impressive.

179

* * *

Besides this cheery idea for a calendar, there were other signs that I was developing a new attitude. The fog that had surrounded me for years was lifting. Part of that fog is the shock of your condition. Part of it is drug-related. Painkillers, sleeping pills, hospital coffee—they all have a foggy effect. The greatest fog inducer, though, is the way other people look at you. Suddenly you are everyone's shining light. You are, for probably the first and only time in your life, a larger-than-life hero.

At first, I saw this as a major asset, worthy of being an early entry in the calendar of daily benefits.

January 3. RELAX! YOU'RE A CERTIFIED DEMI-GOD! YOU SHOULD COMMISSION A BUST OF YOURSELF!

Getting sick gives you special status. It's almost a form of celebrity. A movie star like Brad Pitt or Russell Crowe can leave his wife, make bad movies, throw telephones at hotel clerks, and in general act like a pouty teenager, and it doesn't really matter. Celebrities are exempt from standard rules of conduct and are admired just for being themselves. It's not quite the same for the newly paralyzed, but people do tend to look at you with dewy eyes and cut you a wide behavioral swath. They are just being kind, of course, but a steady diet of adoration is a double-edged sword. Like the over-the-hill actress Norma Desmond in *Sunset Boulevard*, you become hooked on it. It's like the stage gesture of a performer who reacts to applause by acting shy and unworthy while at the same time his or her hands are signaling, "More, more." Adoration feeds the childish need for attention. "You like me, you really like me, and you respect me too!"

Not long after I became sick, here is what the actor, author, pundit, and game show host Ben Stein, an old friend, wrote about me in a column in *American Spectator* magazine:

> *But, in truth, there are many who are braver by far than I. One who zooms immediately to the top of the list is one of my longest-term friends here—Allen Rucker. . . . Allen has never complained about being paralyzed. Never once. He just does his work, supports his family—who also support him—and gets on with it. . . . He's my angel of inspiration on this Christmas Eve.*

Ben is very kind, and I was deeply touched by this sentiment; but "angel of inspiration" is a hard moniker to live up to—especially when you're feeling like the angel of doom. On the other hand, such accolades are seductive. As a way to fend off a constant barrage of self-induced loser thoughts, you start to see yourself as others at least say they see you—a tough nut, someone with the right stuff, one of "the few, the proud," capable of looking calamity in the face and laughing. Get behind me, Satan, I'm rolling here.

This sense of your own special status goes hand in hand with the high drama of becoming paralyzed on a Tuesday afternoon and the heightened anticipation about what might happen next. It's all part of the rush of adrenaline that says you are in a uniquely difficult position and you have the fortitude to survive. And it's a lot better than being told that you are too fragile to handle such a blow, are having a nervous breakdown, and should probably check yourself into a mental hospital or at least an assisted-living facility run by nuns. Your admirers say "heroic." You hear "not an emotional basket case."

A useful consequence of being pegged a role model is that you feel an obligation to live up to the expectations of your cheering squad. When people say, "You are our angel of inspiration," they don't want to hear your pitiful rant about having spent the last two days curled up like a fetus, crying your eyes out. And they don't want to hear you bitch about your sorry career, your late mortgage payment, or problems on the home front. They want to hear gutsy hero talk like: "Paralysis, you know, is no big deal." "I'm going to learn to play wheelchair tennis this weekend. Want to join me?" In fact, as long as you don't do or say anything that is clearly unheroic ("I've become addicted to crack and I love it"), many people will continue to think of you as heroic simply because you are impaired and dealing with it.

"What's the problem?" you ask. Doesn't everyone want to be seen as a hero? Doesn't everyone in America want some form of luminary status, if not his or her own reality TV show, and to be granted the instant admiration usually reserved for firefighters and returning combat veterans?

The problem with elevating the sick to the rank of *Übermensch* is twofold. First, in most cases it's just not true. "Hero," like "celebrity," is an overused, watered-down term and should be reserved for those who endanger their own lives for others. If you become paralyzed in the service of others, then you've earned the right to be called a hero; otherwise, you may be well-regarded but you are still ineligible for hero worship. Second, being called heroic and starting to believe these reports can hinder your return to normality. It's a form of magical thinking. If you buy into it, you begin to think that things will magically work out and—poof!—your sow's ear of a life will be transformed into a beautiful silk purse, hopefully a silk purse full of money. It's like feeling entitled, I guess. "Hey, I suffered this indignity and didn't become a whimpering schnook. I'm entitled to something. Universal veneration will do for a start."

Though I hate to admit it publicly, I am no hero. I am impaired. Being impaired does not automatically confer any status on you, good or bad. In the same way that illness is not a metaphor for a character deficiency or moral error, neither is it a metaphor for greatness or martyrdom. True, some people deal with illness much better than others, and this response may have something to do with their ability to fend off fear, but it has nothing to do with the illness itself. As Dr. Rovner reminded me, people who have, say, a drinking problem before paralysis generally have a drinking problem afterward. Getting ill is just their next rationalization for another bottle of Scotch. The illness itself is an innocent bystander, a physical event with no inherent spiritual dimension.

Of course, there are people who act heroically in the face of illness. Ron Kovic got kicked around and arrested repeatedly for voicing his opposition to the Vietnam war; this was a pretty ballsy thing to do. Christopher Reeve's dedication to finding a cure for paralysis was definitely laudable. There are probably hundreds of less celebrated examples, but they didn't play Superman in the movies or have Barbara Walters's home phone number. Or have Ben Stein as a friend.

Shortly after the onset of my paralysis, there was a good two- or three-month period when I was sure I had undergone a profound expansion of my consciousness and come out the other end more serene and monklike. It was as if I had been sanctified by paralysis. I had been cleansed of ambition, self-centeredness, avarice, and greed. I had ceased to be bothered by the petty irritations of daily life. I was calm, not agitated; forgiving, not resentful; and grateful, not hateful. I was, in a word, cool, for probably the first time in my life. It's as if a couple of months in the hospital and an injury sustained by millions of people around the world had bestowed on me, the good soldier, a dollop of grace.

This didn't last long. It was like falling in love and thinking that all your sins were washed away. Before long, my least monkish behavioral tics began to return. The first time I yelled at a hefty matron for parking in *my* handicapped spot or grimaced at the success of someone else's movie, I knew that my level of grace had slipped back to the subnormal range. Whatever "great awakening" I experienced in the aftermath of paralysis was at best short-lived, and probably more like catatonia than a divine blessing.

Just as the high drama of the ER soon descends into the low, drip-drip drama of reality, the sense that you are special begins to wear off quickly. Others may continue to see you as exemplary, but you yourself are increasingly let down. You've set yourself up for failure. If you bought the hype, the truth of your actual predicament will be all the more painful and your perception of weakness will be all the more acute. You're not a hero, as proclaimed; you're a fraud, a poseur, a faux hero. You are disheartened to find that you still have the same blind spots and the same bank balance one or two years after the onset. If you believed the hype enough to do something silly like take up sand painting or write a spec script about becoming paralyzed, you'll probably end up a bankrupt hero.

I used to announce, for no apparent reason, "Paralysis is not all that it's cracked up to be." No one really laughed at this ironic nonsense, but I kept saying it anyway. One day I realized what the remark meant, at least to me. I really thought, on some level, that paralysis was going to be my ticket out of the ghetto, my moment to excel, my transcendence to being a better person, or just the kick in the ass that I needed to do great things and show the world that I was worthy. And when things didn't happen that way, I was pissed off. It's easy to dismiss someone else's assessment that you are a hero. It's harder to dismiss your own.

Perhaps the greatest single benefit of going through three years of turmoil and coming out on the other side was that I stopped feeling like a victim. This is a real sunny-side effect, worthy of a whole month of cute calendar maxims.

April 13. YOU'LL NEVER AGAIN LOOK INTO A MIRROR AND SAY "LOSER."

April 14. YOU'LL NEVER AGAIN BLAME YOUR MOTHER FOR ALL YOUR PROBLEMS.

April 15. YOUR MOTHER MIGHT BLAME YOU FOR ALL *HER* PROBLEMS, BUT THEN SHE'LL REALIZE YOU'RE IN A WHEELCHAIR AND TAKE IT ALL BACK.

I had never really been a genuine "victim" before all this, but that fact had never stopped me from feeling like one. I saw myself from puberty on as a permanent outsider, and I felt victimized by every misfortune and by a world of strangers who misunderstood me. I was, in least in my own febrile brain, the put-upon, paranoid cowboy Jett Rink, James Dean's character in *Giant*. My only real claim to victimhood was my father's early death, a sad story which probably led to my pose as a loner. In truth, I was an upright, lily-white, Anglo-Saxon, college-educated midwestern male, part of the least marginalized ethnic group in America. I was the stereotype everyone else accused of being the victimizer, not the victim. Except for the fact that I was from Oklahoma and had bow-legs, I'd never been discriminated against in my life.

Still, I saw the world as a victim sees it—I felt the game was rigged. When I came to Hollywood, I came to do battle with con men and hucksters, not make the grade. From the first day I arrived, I felt hoodwinked by the whole Hollywood culture. I was pretty sure these guys would never let me into the club, at the exact same time I was trying everything I could think of to gain entry. I saw show business, the business I desperately wanted to join, as the enemy. I walked into every network pitch meeting with a chip on my shoulder. "If you guys aren't smart enough or gutsy enough to buy this, you are nothing but lowly schlock-meisters." I dressed to make my point—tight jeans, cowboy boots, and a derisive sneer. Would you want to go into business with a guy like that?

The fact that I was of two minds about show business would come out in weird ways. Once, at a meeting at NBC about the pilot for a sitcom, I expressed my displeasure at having to take orders from people I had no respect for by planting my steel-toed boots on the back of a couch, next to the right ear of a network yes-man. I'll sure he was thinking "cauliflower ear," if not "brain damage." Needless to say, the pilot was dropped. Still thinking like a counter-culture idiot, I resented all corporate authority and burned a lot of bridges maintaining my false sense of independence. At one point I got the reputation in some circles as untrustworthy and even unstable, and this cost me some of the best jobs I was ever up for. I had a bad attitude. I had a victim's attitude.

As my so-called career in television went from cable maverick to award-show mercenary, this sense of being treated unfairly grew into a blanket rationale for every failure. The reason couldn't possibly be that, more often than not, I had failed to deliver something either uniquely original or uniquely commercial. No, in my skewed view, it was their fault. It was the system, man, that was keeping me down.

But now, in this wheelchair, I was suddenly a certified, demonstrable victim. I didn't have to announce the fact. It was like a sign hanging from my neck: "Victim of a Cruel Fate." I no longer had to pretend that I had been dealt a crappy hand in life to explain why I couldn't quite get my life in order. I now really had been dealt a crappy hand, a really crappy hand, so don't tell me about your problems, bud. Mine are bigger and, you know, forever!

Many true victims are eager to tell their story, especially in a time where there is a whole media industry devoted to confession and redemption, exemplified by Oprah and Dr. Phil. And a victim's story is usually worth telling, often cathartic for the teller and helpful to others. Victimhood is an altered state of being, and talking about it makes it less fearsome and less isolating. There was a story on the morning news not long ago about a guy who became lost and stranded on the top of a volcano in Hawaii. He immediately started videotaping the experience and continued to do so through three days of fear and desolation. This man was thinking ahead. If he died, the videotape would be a last message to his kids. If he lived, it would be a testament to his survival. At least he wasn't going to die alone and forgotten. His struggle, whatever the outcome, would be on tape.

Being a victim is much different from feeling victimized. Only after attaining the status of a victim did I understand this. Being a true victim is incontrovertible. If a tornado blows down your house, no one is going to say that you had anything to do with it except for your unfortunate decision to settle in the middle of Kansas. If you get breast cancer because your mother got breast cancer, you are a victim. No right-minded person will think, She was a willful, petty woman and had that breast cancer coming.

Feeling victimized, on the other hand, is a precarious position—a state of mind that can be easily challenged. "My son failed math because the teacher doesn't like Asians." "No," a challenger would say, "your son failed math because he was lazy, and then he came up with the excuse that the teacher didn't like Asians." In my own case, my argument would be, "The network people rejected my idea because they didn't want to do business with an outsider like me." The counterargument would be, "No, they simply didn't like the idea. They'd do business with a monkey if they thought it would make a hit TV show. You had nothing to do with it."

There's a huge argument going on in this country as to who's a victim and who's just a whiner. "Victim" is an overused term, like "hero" and "tragedy." Almost anyone with a problem may be described as a victim. Ironically, then, when you actually deserve the title, you don't want it. The last thing you want is to feel victimized. That only makes an unhappy situation worse. Even if a drunk driver ran you over or a bad field commander put you in harm's way, you want to jump up and do something, like beat the guy up or sue. You want to do anything to transcend your general state of helplessness. You're even more inclined to eschew victimhood if you have no one to blame. As Blaine wrote to a friend, "I thank God my dad can't point the finger at a grenade (or any material thing for that matter) and say, 'This thing here. This is why I can't walk. This is why I'm like this.'" You waste a lot less time with spurious finger-pointing if you have nothing and no one to point to but bad luck or a roll of the genetic dice.

When you are permanently disabled, you are victimized, of course, or at least put upon, all the time. But when you are confronted with unacceptable treatment—for instance, no ramp at a restaurant—it makes sense to see this as a discrete moment of inconvenience and nothing more. That's a lot different from the diffuse, self-perpetuating mind-set of victimization, the sense that no matter what you do, you are going to fail because "they" can't help seeing you as a person in a wheelchair. In that mind-set, the cards are permanently stacked against you. Because of something you have no power over, you are excluded for life.

My own dread of always being on the short end of life's stick is gone now. The moment I finally had an excuse for feeling victimized, it no longer seemed like a useful approach to the problem. In the past, if a script buyer called to say, "No, thanks," I could save face by feeling that the system was inherently flawed. But when my legs called and said, "No, thanks," I ran out of systems to blame. In the aftermath, I saw clearly for the first time how I had been bullshitting myself for *two decades* about why I never got a commercial series off the ground or why I never won an Emmy. It's as though the paralysis took my head and shook it until certain ingrained propositions cracked, came apart, and dissipated.

Hopefully, my own persecution complex was abnormally intractable and it doesn't usually take a permanent disability to do away with someone else's. But be on the lookout—this is a very destructive state of mind. It weakens you far more than any physical impairment. I can't really explain the subtle psychological shift from feeling that the whole world is conspiring to ensure your failure to not feeling this way, but I can tell you that it is an indescribably good feeling not to be tormented with the thought. To me, it was akin to an inoculation. The paralysis was like an emotional pathogen introduced into my system to stimulate my defenses against self-pity, anger, and illusions of victimhood. My body, in its new, weird condition, seems to have inspired my mind to overcome some of its own worst habits. I'm sure that, like the urge to smoke a cigarette or drink too much chardonnay, those habits will eventually try for a comeback. But having experienced this momentary liberation, I'll be standing watch.

When you're no longer a hero and no longer a victim, what are you? You're damn close to normal, and it doesn't get scarier than that.

TEN

ALMOST NORMAL

As THE NEW MILLENNIUM APPROACHED, real, practical change began to happen in our lives, not just the fuzzy, inexact permutations of mood and disposition. First, we decided to sell the big house. People sell houses every day, but to us this decision signaled a dramatic change. What had seemed like a painful, and public, admission of failure before the paralysis now seemed like a sensible business decision. At a weak moment a few years earlier, when real estate in California was taking a nosedive, we had contracted with a Realtor to sell the place at whatever price he could wangle. Luckily, we backed out of the deal at the last minute, but before we did, I remember standing in the front yard, alone, looking at the "For Sale" sign and the big two-story neo-midwestern manor behind it and crying as if I had just lost a member of the family. By late 1999, I couldn't imagine crying over a piece of real estate, or at least not this one. The wheelchair had eliminated it from the list of important things.

Purely as a business proposition—and believe me, in southern California, real estate is pure business—we had spent most of the last five or six years pursuing the smartest market strategy we could have regarding the house. We did nothing, though not because we were savvy business types with impeccable timing and nerves of steel. We did nothing because we were scared and trapped. But given the shifting marketplace, our almost pathological inability to act became our saving grace. Now, if we were lucky, we could sell this too-much-house for a tidy profit; buy a smaller house with a smaller mortgage; and perhaps right our listing ship, which had been taking on water since Reagan was president.

Also, we hated the place, or at least Ann hated it. It represented to her every bad thing that had happened in the previous ten-plus years. It was like the house in *The Shining*, full of spirits and ghosts that would drive anyone insane. I'm sure she thought I'd show up at the bathroom door some night, meat cleaver in hand, announcing, "Heeeeere's Johnny!" She came to see the house as so filled with bad memories that even if a fortune had dropped out of the sky, she would never be happy living there. To her, it was forever too big, too pretentious, and a false representation of our life.

The house wasn't too big for my tastes, but I understood its costs, both financial and emotional. I understood that Ann and I were estranged and unhappy, stuck in two distant wings of this airy manor every night. I had once thought the house was a logical precursor to a large, secure life, in the same way that a young go-getter in Hollywood will lease a Mercedes he can't afford so that the world will see him as a success and treat him as such. It doesn't work that way. I never got a fat deal because I lived in a big house.

Because of my upbringing, I had an inordinate attachment to houses. My mother clung to our family home in Bartlesville, Oklahoma, where she and her husband had planted their stake. It was a connection to her happiest days. To her, the address, 1429 Valley Road, had the romantic punch of 10 Downing Street or 79 Park Avenue. After she was finally forced to sell it, she never again found a real home, and I was afraid the same destiny awaited me. I thought I was stuck in a family script in which I was to repeat my mother's slow descent from rich doctor's wife to homeless renter.

I harbored that fear until the day when reality finally strolled in and slapped me across the face. "It's a freaking house, you idiot—wood, plumbing, central air—and it's a major pain in the butt. It's screwing with your life. Lose it!"

I realized that in gleefully deciding to unload the house, I had already unloaded the expectations that the house symbolized. I no longer worried about playing catch-up with much more successful Hollywood friends who had started out in the same $85-a-month off-campus apartment. Nor was I interested in continuing to promote a mainstream show business career I knew I didn't have and wasn't likely to attain in this lifetime. I stopped going to movies and walking out saying, "I can write a funnier script than that"—and then going home to spend days trying to come up with a killer movie premise to pitch. Or a killer sitcom premise. Or even a killer reality show or talk show or game show premise. The paralysis was a clear demarcation between that twenty-year phase of often misplaced energy and the rest of my life. Selling the house was simply unloading excess baggage.

We probably should have left LA even before the paralysis and found a less stressful way to live; but we had nowhere to go and I still had a career here, however checkered. I didn't share the common sentiment that there is more happiness to be found in "real life" than in the hurly-burly world of Hollywood. My life was real enough right here. I was a little worried about how to spin all this downsizing, as if anyone besides me cared. In the end, I didn't have to make any excuses. Scaling back after becoming paralyzed seemed like good sense, not failure.

Having decided to operate within sane limits, physical and financial, the next question to be answered was: what *was* I going to do for the rest of my life? My career as a writer of television specials was leveling off, at least for the time being. A few people in that business kept calling, but a list too long to print here didn't call, for whatever reason. The producers Tony Eaton and Dan Harris hauled me off to wheelchair-averse places like the Texas Motor Speedway to do shows and finally to Monte Carlo and the Côte d'Azur for a big international gala, the *Laureus Sports Awards*. Tiger Woods couldn't make it, but a strange amalgam of celebrities including Venus and Serena Williams, Naomi Judd, Jon Bon Jovi, and Nelson Mandela answered the bell. The German sponsors didn't like us, so we weren't invited back, but it was the grandest TV trek I ever made, wheelchair and all.

My career was at another crossroads. It seemed as if the "Make it by fifty" rule was about to be invoked and the Show Business Bouncer was about to show me the door. I'm sure that if I had redoubled my efforts to hustle short-term gigs and to schmooze producers, I could have kept up the appearance of being a player. There are people in Hollywood who luck into a one-shot show every two or three years and consider themselves players. "Didn't you see that Paul Anka thing I did in 1998? I'm talking to him about something else.... He's a piece of work, you know...." This is the Land of BS, and a lot of it goes on in interior monologues. After all, all it takes is one lucky break, one roll of the dice, and you're a senior writer on *Dancing with the Stars* or *Growing Up Gotti* and back in circulation. "I know I'll make it. I just need a break, damn it." That's what thousands of people are telling themselves this morning in Hollywood.

But, hey, sometimes you do get a break. I was lucky, through an awards show, to meet the programmers at the cable network TNT. At that point, TNT had an active nonfiction division, turning out cultural documentaries with themes related to the history of entertainment. In the business, these are derisively called "clip shows." They use a lot of archival material from movies, stills, and the news; and in quality they can range from slapdash celebrity bios to evocative, thoughtful pieces about, say, the Civil War or the history of New York. Writing a historical documentary usually consists of composing off-camera interview questions and on-camera voice-over narration to help keep the story on track. Many devotees of the form hate voice-over narration because it's often done badly, and even more often, very badly. When it is overapplied, as is usually the case, it's writing that points to itself—"As the ancient Greeks once surmised ..."—and it can turn a kinetic film experience into a radio-with-a-screen illustrated lecture.

The programmers at TNT asked me to help write a history of the western movie, and it came out well. James Garner narrated, and he's the kind of charming pro where anything that comes out of his mouth sounds good. As with Walter Cronkite, give him a grocery list and he'll fill it with gravitas. Anyway, TNT liked the show, *Big Guns Talk*; it won an award or two; and soon the network had another similar documentary in mind—one that would compare mob movies, one of the most successful genres in filmdom, with the real life of real mobsters. Produced and directed by the award-winning filmmakers Joe and Sandra Consentino, the film would search for the line where the movies stopped and reality began. As it turned out, that line wasn't easy to find.

I first had to remind TNT that I was from a small midwestern town, not Little Italy. The closest I'd ever gotten to anything remotely Italian before the age of eighteen was canned Franco-American spaghetti, and *The Untouchables* on television on Thursday nights. I thought Parmesan cheese came only in Kraft's containers with the little holes in the top. Why did TNT want a heartlander like me to write a mob doc? I suggested that they find a writer from Bayonne, but they said no, I was the guy. As any self-respecting Guido would answer, "Hey, whadda ya gonna do?" I said thank you and started watching old James Cagney movies.

Joe Consentino had a brilliant idea, one of many. He found a loose collection of actors in the New York area who specialized in character roles in mob movies. Back in the late 1990s, you might not recognize their names, but you'd seen their faces so often you could identify them in a lineup by their screen roles. "Oh, yeah, you're Billy Batts, the dead guy from *Goodfellas*" (Frank Vincent). "Oh, sure, I remember you; you played Angelo 'Quack-Quack' Ruggerio in *Gotti*" (Vincent Pastore). "Aren't you the badass from *Analyze This*?" (Tony Darrow).

This group of mob-centric actors even had a name for themselves—the Gangsters Actors Guild (GAG). They became kind of a Greek chorus for our documentary, which was called *Family Values: The Mob and the Movies*. Although only a few members of GAG had a criminal record (one, named Mike "Scuch," had beaten a guy to death with a baseball ball), they all came from the right mob-infested neighborhoods—Brooklyn, East New York, New Rochelle—and knew the daily, often mundane, details of this highly mythologized life. Especially when they appeared in the fact-based mob films of Martin Scorsese, they often personally knew the real-life characters they played on-screen. Together, they were an invaluable source for everything from the day Joe Columbo got it in broad daylight at Columbus Circle to why "men of respect" (i.e., mobsters) are still respected on Eighth Avenue in Bensonhurst.

Joe Consentino, along with GAG, brought me into a world that the movies had barely touched. Joe made contact with a great, Bensonhurst-born crime reporter, Jerry Capeci, who knew and described real New York mobsters as if they were his next-door neighbors, which wasn't far from the truth. John Gotti? "A hijacker from Queens ... a degenerate gambler." The Mafia code? "For the most part they are killers without any honor at all."

Capeci knew his stuff. He had cowritten (with Gene Mustain) the book on Gotti used as the basis for the HBO movie

Gotti. But even closer to the black heart of "the life," he had chronicled, again with Mustain, probably the most depraved, animalistic group the New York mob ever turned out. The book is entitled *Murder Machine* and the crew was a band of merry psychopaths headed up by a Brooklyn capo named Roy DeMeo.

These guys, operating in the cocaine-heyday of the seventies, blow every *Godfather*-tinged fairy tale about the mob out of the water. The DeMeo crew killed people, maybe hundreds of them, for hire, sure, but also for fun. They ran a place above a bar in Brooklyn that was dubbed the Horror Hotel. You walked up some stairs, entered a room with a tarp on the floor, got stuck in the heart with a knife or shot in the head with a gun, and were hung up in the shower to bleed while the crew ordered in pizza. You were then butchered, bagged, and sent to the dump in a friendly carting truck. Once this reality sinks in, any reader would cease to describe himself as a "mob lover."

At the core of the film *Family Values* were stories of real-life people like Roy DeMeo and ex-mobsters like Dominick Montiglio, a foot soldier turned "in the wind" informer whose uncle was an underboss in the Gambino family. The movie clips provided dramatic counterpoint, and the gangster actors made it all seem perfectly believable, almost normal. During the shooting of the film, two of the performers from GAG kept talking about a pilot they were involved in that they were sure was destined to be one of the primo depictions of mob life ever made. These two performers were Tony Sirico and Vincent Pastore. After that pilot aired, television viewers soon came to know them as "Paulie Walnuts" and "Big Pussy." The show was *The Sopranos*.

If you asked David Chase of *The Sopranos* how to succeed in Hollywood, he'd tell you that luck is as big a factor as any. "If you have a hit show of any kind," he once said, "even a *bad* hit show, but especially to have a hit that you love ... that's an infinitesimally small target to hit. What luck." My luck, at this confusing time in my life, was knowing David Chase. We had met first in 1969, when I entered the Stanford Graduate Film Program, a small program concentrating largely on documentaries. David was already there, along with John Patterson, who would become one of the principal directors of *The Sopranos* and who recently died of prostate cancer. Chase soon left for Hollywood and became a wunderkind in episodic television drama, writing and producing grade-A shows including *The Rockford Files*, *Northern Exposure*, and *I'll Fly Away*. I went on to my spotty career in fringe television. We kept in touch and occasionally had lunch, but we seemed to operate in different showbiz spheres. In other words, for the most part, he had a career and I had a series of jobs.

Tony Sirico ("Paulie Walnuts") showed the documentary *Family Values* to Chase, who called to congratulate me. I was out of work at the time, and I steered the conversation (oh so smoothly) to, "Listen, old friend, if there is anything I might be right for on your new show ..." He replied, "Hey, would you be interested in writing a *Sopranos* companion book?" Not knowing what a companion book actually was, I said, "Absolutely, count me in, I'm there."

I didn't believe Chase for a minute—there had to be a hundred well-connected people in Hollywood lined up for the plum assignment of writing a *Sopranos* book—but a few months later I got a call from his manager, Susie Fitzgerald. I was sky-high. A checkered résumé that had included, at one time or another, handmade documentaries, music videos, sketch comedy, sitcoms, television movies, award shows, clip shows, and *The World's Worst Drivers* was now taking another curious turn—television tie-in books. This is not the kind of career move you dream about in film school, but, hey, who wouldn't want to be associated with *The Sopranos*?

The book we put together, *The Sopranos: A Family History*, was not an exercise in *Access Hollywood*–style celebrity fawning and puffery. ("What does James Gandolfini really like in a woman?") Staying within the lines of the show, and with Chase's guidance, I was free to fill in the blanks and invent any plausible extrapolation I wanted. In the spirit of a mock volume like *The History of White People in America*, only a little bloodier, the book became a faux history of this faux mob family, complete with faux family photos, faux rap sheets, faux psychiatry notes, and Meadow's faux Discover card invoice. *The Sopranos* is so richly detailed as a television show that extending the saga back to a small village in the province of Avellino in southern Italy or forward to a newspaper article in Newark announcing the disappearance of Salvatore "Big Pussy" Bonpensiero was a gas. It was a different type of comedy posing as reality.

Companion or tie-in books related to television series are not highly regarded by anyone save publishers and fans. They are way, way down the literary ladder, at around the same rung as celebrity workout books and the Paris Hilton oeuvre. You will never see a blurb from the *New York Times* saying, "Best companion book since *Will and Grace*! Way better than *According to Jim*!" Never having written a companion book, I didn't know how low the bar was set and felt no hesitancy about stooping to the genre, as long as I could do something marginally original. Trust me, I had sunk lower than a mock-journalistic take on the best show on television. Much lower.

This detailed chronicle of "your contemporary mob family" leaned on the research of a fictional, self-important authority on the Mafia, Jeffrey Wernick, author of such classics as "La Cosa Nostra: A Children's Guide to Our Thing" and "He's My F**kin' Brother—Kinship Patterns in Mob Life." Wernick's files included everything from an analysis by the FBI of the Sopranos' garbage—"one (1) half-eaten baked ziti casserole with refrigerator mold"—to a letter of support from Tony's high school English teacher bemoaning the fact that "Anthony has no ethical guide dog." The book was also an opportunity to describe what real mobsters do on a daily basis, the "trickle-up" economics of loan-sharking and construction racketeering, just in case readers were interested in setting up their own mob operation.

In the end, I realized that I had derived more pleasure from writing this one piece of tie-in merchandising than from writing a hundred television scripts. I had only one or two people to answer to, not a roomful of humor-challenged television execs or movie stars. Writing was again something I looked forward to rather than dreaded. I'd hate to call tie-in books my métier, but this one was closer to my creative wheelhouse than a lifetime of specials like *Mickey's Very Very Merry Christmas*.

The Sopranos: A Family History did fine, riding the obvious Big Kahuna of a show now being called the best television drama ever made. On the basis of the book, I became part of the *Sopranos* family, a kind of distant cousin who wrote inside-the-family web reports (jefferywernick.com); created original online video vignettes like a cheesy late-night television commercial for Nuovo Vesuvio restaurant; and answered trivia questions from morning drive-time radio shock jocks when no one in the cast or crew would return their calls. I went to *Sopranos* premieres and Emmy parties and finally had something to tell people who asked, "So, what have you been up to lately, besides, you know, the paralysis?" I began to feel again like a not-quite-but-almost-maybe-could-be-it's-not-too-late creative player.

The Sopranos is a genuine television gusher, and some of that oil started to fall on my head. The next book project, thought up by God knows who, was *The Sopranos Family Cookbook*. A brilliant food writer, Michele Scicolone, a native of Brooklyn, was brought in to compile a hundred recipes for southern Italian dishes that the *Sopranos* characters had eaten on the show or could theoretically order from Artie Bucco's ristorante. I was brought in to give the book a *Soprano*-esque twist. The twist was obvious: a cookbook compiled by Artie Bucco himself after watching Emeril on the Food Channel and envying his success. This was something Artie could promote all over the tristate area and maybe drum up a few more dinner reservations.

So Artie wrote the introduction to the book, chose his favorite Neapolitan dishes (like "Osso Buco alla Bucco"), and persuaded his closest friends in New Jersey to contribute their thoughts about every Italian-American's favorite topic, food. Tony's sister, Janice, for instance, describes the Sunday dinners of their youth, which always degenerated into their father deriding their mother's overcooked pork as "Particle Board Alla Livia." Furio, the thug imported from Naples, calls drinking cappuccino after dinner something only "Germans" would do, the insult of insults. Big man Bobby Bacala weighs in on the "cult of thinness" that is ruining America's youth, along with "Style Tips for Heavy Eaters." (Rule 1: No tank tops.)

The tongue-in-cheek cookbook format conjoined with the name *Sopranos* was a tie-in dream come true. Released in late 2002, *The Sopranos Family Cookbook* became number one on the *New York Times* miscellany best-seller list and stayed there for weeks. It was the perfect Christmas gift for a goombah-wannabe in the family and, in a series of foreign-language editions, even for goombahs speaking Swedish, Hungarian, or Korean. The idea of someone in Seoul sitting down to read AJ Soprano's middle-school essay, "Why I Like Food," and whipping up a batch of "Quail Sinatra Style with Fennel Sausage" continues to, you know, blow my mind, man.

In November of that year, a cartoonist for the *New York Times Book Review*, Mark Alan Stamaty, devoted his full-page strip, "Boox," to satirizing a book so perfectly attuned to the commercial marketplace. The strip begins with a first-time writer thrilled beyond words that his or her book is actually getting published as he or she dreams of the riches of bestseller-dom. A few panels later the book is in the remainders box at a bookstore while Stamaty posits that to sell a book these days, you've got to have a hook, like *The Sopranos Family Cookbook*. He goes on to wave other such books in the poor writer's face, like "The Sopranos Guide to Interior Decorating." The message: this is the kind of shameless, can't-lose merchandising that "real" book writers have to compete with.

For the first time in my life, something I was involved in was being crucified on the cross of rank commercialism. And

I loved it! In thirty years of cranking out media works of all forms, I had never done anything that had even come close to hitting the commercial radar. I have had my share of cult successes, and I treasure them all; but I had long been convinced that I was genetically uncommercial. The late comic novelist Stanley Elkin (author of *The Magic Kingdom*), a brilliant writer who never found an audience on the scale of Philip Roth's, once said that he felt a tinge of regret when he was on an airplane and sat next to someone who asked, "Would I be familiar with any of your books?" He knew the answer was no. He wrote dozens of books, won dozens of awards, but never wrote anything that made it into everyday vernacular like *Portnoy's Complaint* or Joseph Heller's *Catch–22*. If you do good work and only four people know about it, and that's your whole career, that's painful.

Since I liked the cookbook and thought it was pretty funny, I was delighted that it had made the comic pages of the *New York Times Book Review*, even if it was being derided. I had proved something to myself, or something had been proved to me. I knew now that other material I would write, and feel assured in writing, had a chance. If writing is in some degree a confidence game, I had just won myself over. It might not make sense to anyone else, but writing those two *Sopranos* books was an epiphany, or maybe two epiphanies, I don't exactly know how those things are measured. After thirty years of working in television, and having started over six or seven times, I was starting over again.

Around the time we decided to sell the house and the *Sopranos* bandwagon began, my correspondence with Kit Sibert, which had lasted more than two years, started to taper off. Long before I actually felt rosier, I presented, in writing, a rosy picture to her, in detail: "A smaller, one-story house, a new career path that mixes less showbiz and more teaching, more free time to f**k around, letting my mind really work for a change . . ." Except for the more teaching, I was right on track. For her part, Kit was beginning to change as well, writing, painting, and throwing herself back into social work. As she wrote to me, recovery was an ever-so-slow process, but life was starting to "seduce" her back. In the fall of 2000, she had an art show in Eugene and sold a good number of paintings. Earlier that year, we worked together on a reading in Los Angeles for her late husband Jody's now published book, *Toil*. A big crowd turned out to praise both Jody and Kit. It was a fitting and lasting tribute to Kit's toil as much as Jody's.

But Kit continued to keep me honest long after I announced to her that I had "recovered." Because her husband's death had happened well after my paralysis, her own sorrow and confusion were still very much present. At one point she wrote that she thought it took five years to recover from such a loss and "the longer away it gets, the more private becomes the suffering, so it gets lonelier." She went on: "I don't think we 'get over' these things. They just keep stunning us in different ways, at different angles, in different places." At the time she wrote this, I was sure the weight that had been lifted from me was long gone. Of course it wasn't, and every time it reappeared, it stunned me at a different angle and I was surprised all over again.

A year or so later, Kit announced that a certain "robustness" had finally come back into her life, a sure sign that her own black cloud had lifted. Looking back, we still wonder exactly what purpose we served for each other at the juncture of my paralysis and her widowhood. Kit's word for it is "confirmation." She felt awful; and I said, fine, feel awful, feel very awful, and while you're at it, get a load of this dung heap of misery and regret. I would never have raised my hand at a paralysis recovery support group and talked about my sorry emotional condition, but with Kit it was a piece of cake. My advice to anyone going through a severe medical crisis: find a single confidant with a huge heart. I know I would have been at a terrible loss in those early years without the compassion, whining, patience, pity-potty-ing, sarcasm, commiseration, and good sense of Kit Sibert.

In early 2000, the new millennium well under way, our big house was ready for sale. Both Ann and I threw ourselves into sprucing it up and clearing away a garageful of accumulated stuff, and this coordinated effort became the first step in returning to a life and a marriage that had preceded not only the paralysis but the whole awful decade of the 1990s. It was time to get out and start over.

The house sold in two hours on a Sunday afternoon for more than the asking price, and three days before it officially went on the market. Welcome to LA. As luck (again) would have it, Ann-Marie spotted another house nearby the first morning it had a sign in front of it, and we bought it the next day. It was more our style. It was all of 900 square feet, but had a lovely pool and a vine-strewn pergola in the backyard. Moving there was like going from a real house to a vacation cabin. Given the radical reduction in living space, we sold or gave away two-thirds of our furnishings. We saw decades of our life go down the street in the back of the donations truck sent by Hope Lutheran Church and felt hardly a tinge of regret.

Our new street in West LA had no sidewalks or curbs, and if you squinted, you could imagine that you were on a country road in the middle of Metropolis. The front of the house looked like small-town Mississippi. The back looked like an afternoon in rural Italy. Ann later said that making the move felt like the biggest accomplishment of her life, and I knew exactly what she meant. It was a genuine change in our interior and exterior lives. We had finally arrived at a place of real comfort, in every way. We were all living in one small space, face-to-face if not elbow to elbow. We had pared away so much of our former life that in Ann's mind we were like the family in the Swedish classic *The Immigrants*. We'd packed up only the most essential things—a few photos, Grandma's favorite tablecloth—and moved on to a new life in a new land, a good two and a half miles away.

Ann-Marie and I were back to sleeping in the same bed and sharing the same life. We were also back to freely expressing the ardor we had set aside for years. We weren't exactly Ozzie and Harriet, and we never will be, but being together again was easy, affectionate, and mutually supportive. It is a truism that tragedy or illness is always harder on the nearest loved one than on the victim himself. I don't know how you gauge these things, but the whole ordeal tested Ann-Marie as much as or more than anyone else; and I am forever thankful, and mindful, that her love, caring, courage, and competence got us both through those dark years.

Our new house brought back memories of the first apartment we rented as newlyweds. We could afford the rent then and we could handle the mortgage now. More important, we now had the cash to pay everyone we owed. Even the IRS sent a nice thank-you letter. More than ten years of pain, confusion, self-incrimination, and bad feelings went out in the afternoon mail. All that stress, all that worry, all that arguing night after night about what we were going to do, all those dunning notices and late fees and lawyers' letters and not-so-friendly friendly-reminder phone calls at dinnertime—all were gone within forty-eight hours after the close of escrow.

Talk about your happy endings.

ELEVEN

LIFE AFTER PARALYSIS

I HATE BEING PARALYZED. I hate every minute of it. Every time it dawns on me that I can't do something like swing on a passing tree limb or take Blaine or Max down for a three count in the backyard, it's like a stab in the gut. Then there are those moments of sadness and regret that come back again and again, usually at night, usually triggered by some real-world occurrence like seeing myself in a full-length mirror in a department store. Feeling whipped by the paralysis has become a phenomenon that occurs every six weeks or so. Thank goodness that this slough of depression and self-pity comes and goes with some regularity. Otherwise, this whole book would be a real downer, like *Leaving Las Vegas* or *Police Academy 6*.

Here's an example of what could trigger this depression: The TNT biopic *George Wallace* came out the first year after

I became paralyzed. The actor Gary Sinese was brilliant as Wallace, the "race and rage" governor of Alabama who became a southern icon. Readers born after 1970 may not know about Wallace, a charismatic segregationist. He professed to hate Washington but nevertheless ran for president; while campaigning, he was shot in the back and spent the rest of his life in a wheelchair. There was an image in the film that I will take to the big nursing home in the sky. Late in the story, Wallace and his second wife, Cornelia, played by Angelina Jolie, are alone in the governor's mansion in Alabama. They are listening to the legendary country singer Patsy Cline, and in a gesture of wifely seduction, Cornelia drapes her arm awkwardly around George's neck and tries to dance with him in his wheelchair. "I can't dance," George says. Still, they try a spin or two, and then Cornelia attempts to arouse George with a tender lap dance. George's reaction is a painful spasm that, uh, breaks the mood. Up to that point, George has been blank-faced. This little episode isn't fun for him. It's heartbreaking and humiliating.

What stayed with me was the charade of a wheelchair user trying to dance. When I see someone in a chair or otherwise disabled having to strain to appear "normal," I myself feel inadequate, embarrassed, and resentful. Unless these gestures are just good-natured jokes, they are at best inauthentic and at worst condescending. Another example occurred on Jerry Lewis's telethon years ago, when the great football player Joe Namath was a guest. Lewis decided to have Broadway Joe throw a pass onstage to one of "Jerry's kids" who had muscular dystrophy. The kid went along with this travesty and stood there bravely. When Namath reared back and pitched a spiral from ten yards away, it hit the kid square in the chest and bounced off. Everybody applauded to cover their mortification. It was cruel and pathetic.

I've seen choreographed performances involving people lifted from their wheelchairs and carried aloft by an able-bodied dance partner as if they were soaring on their own momentum. Others surely see this as daring and courageous. Sitting in a chair, I flinch. Dancing, something I wasn't particularly skilled at doing before I was paralyzed, is movement, spontaneous full-body movement, whether it involves shuffling around to Marvin Gaye or sneaking up behind your wife and embracing her or climbing stairs two at a time. But when you have no legs, or no use of your legs, you can't dance. And that's that.

This doesn't mean you should stay in bed all day or phone in your regrets to the invitations committee from your high school reunion because you're unable to reprise the funky chicken on cue. Being too squeamish about taking risks may keep you from trying things like adaptive skiing or handicapped bowling. Avoiding such activities would be stupid, of course, since people in wheelchairs can ski and bowl, and doing so is neither fraudulent nor pathetic. Well, skiing could be pathetic if you keep falling on your face in the snow, but you'll get high marks for trying.

The problem for chair users is feeling pressured to do things you think are unwise, or just uncomfortable, in order to keep up a hearty appearance. If you are in no condition or mood to ski, bowl, or get down on the dance floor, just roll away. It's your God-given right to just be paralyzed. You don't need the stress of being super-paralyzed. Tell yourself, "I'm a paralytic but not a very good one." You have nothing to prove. Paralysis isn't a contact sport or a race to sainthood.

This kind of thinking runs counter to the aggressive ethos

of the "new disabled," the mind-set where "can't" is the rally cry for "Screw you, the hell I can't, jerk-off!" to every possible challenge conjured up in *New Mobility* or *Sports 'n' Spokes*. If you're twenty-nine, or think you're twenty-nine, maybe that's the mind-set to have. On the other hand, you just might find that operating *inside* your limitations could be liberating. It might free you from really thinking you're not good enough to encounter the world on your own terms.

Susan Sontag opens "Illness as Metaphor" by delineating two worlds: the kingdom of the sick and the kingdom of the well. Somewhere between these two domains lies an often chaotic, ill-governed nation-state: the kingdom of the old. No one wants to go there. Most people I know deny that the kingdom of the old even exists, at least with regard to their own lives, in the same way that seasoned mobsters will look at you with a straight face and claim that there is no such thing as a Mafia. Sixty is the new forty, eighty the new forty-five, blah, blah, blah. This national conspiracy to market the aged as reconstituted teenagers—"It's great to be silver!"— seems to be working. "Ten Ways to Stay Young!" shout the promos for morning television shows. "Way number 3: Stay hip! Do young-people things like watching *Fear Factor* and IM'ing your grandkids! Dress like Snoop!"

According to a report in *American Demographics* on a survey done in 2002, half of all baby boomers are depressed because they are aging, and nearly one in five admits to actively resisting aging. In 2002, most boomers were in their mid-forties or younger. They were not even close to old, and they were already discombobulated by the idea of old age.

When I became paralyzed, I felt as if I were getting old fast, a front-runner in the race toward decrepitude and death.

I'm sure this feeling had something to do with the fact that some people treated me as older, which I hated, or that I was spending so much time in hospital beds, surrounded by infirm seniors. It took me a while to return to the pat but true notion of my own generation that getting old in the conventional sense of reducing my pace to a slow walk, going to discount movies in the middle of the week, or, God forbid, retiring, was nonsense, whether or not I was in a wheelchair. In many ways I am no different from what I was the day I became paralyzed. I try to slip in a short nap every day—fatigue goes with my condition—but I'm still at my workstation as much as or more than ever; and I see absolutely no reason to adapt to a paralytic lifestyle, whatever that is. I gave up on merengue lessons and the dream of hiking up the Himalayas in search of the elusive snow leopard, but neither of those things, as exciting as they might seem, were central to my existence. If I hadn't become paralyzed, I would have come up with some other excuse not to do them.

But I am permanently impaired, permanently physically compromised, and that fact has allowed me at least a weekend pass into the kingdom of the old. There are ground rules for being there, ground rules that, I promise, will not sit well with the generation raised on the William Blake adage "The road of excess leads to the palace of wisdom." The "experience junkies" of the 1960s and their younger counterparts don't like the concept of limits. It's an attack on their personal freedom. They've never been down the road of caution and moderation, which probably leads to the palace of oatmeal. They've never settled for less than enough. Until, that is, they get seriously sick or injured. Then, all of a sudden, they stop seeing themselves as twenty-nine.

Actually, even in the face of such a blow, many don't get the message. At least, I didn't. After only a few months away from the hospital I forgot the harsh lessons of the pulmonary embolism that had almost done me in, and I returned to my pre-paralysis view that I was chronologically fifty-five but in every other way thirty-five. Paralysis, I fell back to thinking, is like age—just a state of mind, a way to excuse apathy and indolence. No, it's not. It's an altered physical state that demands you give it respect or it will kick you in the keister. Hard.

In late 2001, well into year five of my paralysis and feeling spunky, I went to Oklahoma to visit my mother on her ninetieth birthday. The whole trip, in my mind, loomed as an exercise in maximum mobility. I rented a car with hand controls at the Tulsa airport and drove around the state like a madman, on my own schedule and under my own power. I drove a couple of hundred miles to Oklahoma City and back in a day to have lunch with my dearest high school friends. I drove up to Bartlesville, my hometown, the next day to see my sister Louise, then hightailed it back to Tulsa for a book interview. Driving is big in the plains states. People think nothing of getting on the road for two or three hours to visit in-laws and then drive back home again. My brother has kids who will speed up and back from Dallas on a Sunday just to see his new tractor. It's a way of life.

So that's what I did. I embraced a four-day stint of white-line fever and mediocre country radio. I didn't have time to rest, and by the time I returned to Los Angeles, I was exhausted. Big deal—take a nap. I took a three-hour nap and woke up with a temperature of 103, diarrhea, nausea, and just a spot of trepidation. My right ankle had what we thought was a garden-variety pressure sore that was reasonably under control. But when I awoke with the fever, it was bright red. I chalked the inflammation up to the long airplane ride, figured that I was just beat or that maybe I'd eaten too much Okie beef, and fell asleep again.

Twelve hours later I was in the Cedars ER with a temperature of 105 and a right leg as swollen as a country ham and red up to the knee. No worry. Just put me in bed with intravenous antibiotics, as had happened a half dozen times before, and I'd be home in no time. The antibiotics went in, but the fever didn't go away. It got worse, continually spiking night and day at 102 to 104, and accompanied by chills and sweats. The discomfort of being constantly feverish was maddening. Old standbys like Motrin and Extra-Strength Tylenol were useless. When the fever spiked in the high range, the nurses would bring ice bags for under my arms and behind my neck. When ice didn't bring it down, out came an instrument of torture called a cooling blanket, an ice-filled bottom sheet that got down to 38 degrees. If my whole body could have felt it, I would have freaked out. As it was, only my shoulders felt frozen; my teeth chattered, just as in the cartoons; and I got through the cooling.

After a few days of this, the medical team got worried. An MRI showed subdermal decay in my leg. Bacteria were working on my muscle tissue, and they had yet to be stopped by the heavy-duty antibiotics. These microbes had a name: necrotizing fasciitis. "Necrotizing" means "make dead" and "fasciitis" refers to the fat and tissue covering the leg muscle. "Make tissue dead" is the general idea.

Newscasters on television have a catchier term for this bug: flesh-eating bacteria. As in: "Deadly flesh-eating bacteria are chewing their way through the trailer parks of southern Arizona and should hit Palm Springs by nightfall." Along with killer bees and coyotes that eat your cat, the specter of flesh-eating Pac men invading your body is a surefire headline-grabber in southern California. And it's a fun term to hear doctors mumble outside the door of your hospital room. The redness on my leg had now climbed to the crotch area, but the decay had yet to spread beyond the lower calf. No one had given me a definitive prognosis, but they were round-ing up specialists right and left. I was just happy that they had come up with something, however nasty-sounding, to account for the agonizing fever.

The next morning a doctor operated on the leg and de-brided the infected area. This seemed like progress. I now hoped to be home after a stay of "only" ten to twelve days. (My Munchausen's-by-Paralysis love of hospitals, by the way, had turned to revulsion around the second day of the high fever.) My temperature started spiking lower (at 101 to 103); and after another day or so, the leg started changing colors and the swelling subsided. Still, things didn't seem quite right. I didn't feel much better. A constant fever, even a low-grade fever, can suck the spirit right out of you. I felt that the hospital stay itself was starting to make me sick, or at least adding to my sickness. I had to get out.

Finally, by the thirteenth day, I was back home with a semipermanent IV feeder in my arm, called a peripherally inserted central catheter (PICC) line. A visiting nurse came in daily to check on my progress. This was all good except for one thing: I still had a recurring fever. It now seemed as if I would be overheated for the rest of my life. No one could fig-ure out what was the matter, until one doctor speculated that I had "drug fever," a feverish reaction caused by the antibiotics themselves. He suggested removing the IV. Fine with me. They pulled it out, and I slowly got better. I never received a definitive explanation as to why I had been sick for so long. It was either drug fever or maybe yet another infection caused by the PICC line in my upper arm. Such are the mysteries of modern medicine.

Coming when it did, years after I thought I was out of the woods, this health crisis was a lesson in caution for me. My thinking took a decided turn: I now had to assume, for sanity's sake, that I would never again be "not sick." I was not constantly ill or totally incapacitated, but I had entered a place, mostly populated by old people, where getting sick is an ever-present possibility. There was now a precariousness to my existence that I had to own up to. There's the obvious precariousness of spending your life on four rubber wheels; but even more, you know that a slight nick or scratch on a part of your body you can't feel could lead to some bug eating your leg muscle. You're particularly vulnerable—a fact that you have to ignore and pay attention to at the same time. If you only ignore it, you could lose a leg or worse. If you constantly pay attention to it, you cease to function in the world. At that point, in my opinion, you are officially old.

And the minute you think nothing is going to happen again, something happens. One Friday morning a good three and a half years after this brush with necrotizing fasciitis, I spotted a patch of red on the inside of my right calf. Three hours later I was back in the ER, temperature rising. Because of my previous problem in the same leg, the staff took a CAT scan and then exchanged worried looks, called in a surgeon, and wheeled me into the operating room. This time on the way to surgery, Ann and I overheard a doctor mumble, "May

217

have to cut it off." May have to cut it off? As scary as that sounds, for the first time in my life it didn't seem like a completely insane idea. The leg made me feel like a whole person, but it really didn't have much function in my life except as a breeding ground for nasty bacteria.

The surgeon took a goodly slab of flesh out of my calf in the belief that necrotizing fasciitis was at work again. Much to everyone's surprise, he didn't find any. The wound was left open for a couple of days, just in case; then the calf was stapled back together and I was pronounced out of danger. The fever continued for another week—some kind of bacteria were at work somewhere. It finally abated, though not before I had another round of antibiotic toxicity that made my life miserable.

The moral of this story: it never ends. If your health has been seriously compromised, get used to it. "Act your age," my mother used to chide. Since probably no one reading this book plans on doing that, then we'll modify it to: act your condition. Don't let it get you down, but never again think that you are young and stupid and can continue to operate with flippant disdain for the pitfalls of illness and aging. The life you lose may be your own.

What will happen when not just thousands but millions of people contract certain diseases as they age—cancer, Parkinson's disease, diabetes, MS, and even, occasionally, transverse myelitis? The raw demographics—76 million baby boomers, someone turning fifty every seven seconds, one in four Americans over sixty by 2030, 16 million with Alzheimer's by 2050, etc.—favor a major growth spurt in all kinds of age-related health care, not to mention the fields of wheelchair manufacturing, bladder management, memory restoration, and hopefully books like this. As has been widely reported by everyone hoping to cash in on this marketing bonanza, we're about to enter the Age of Aging.

I for one am rooting for this new age to take hold soon, because A, I'm aging and B, I currently feel estranged from most people my age and look forward to again appearing, by comparison, ordinary. I hope that the compulsion to dye our collective hair and keep looking backward will fade as we all get comfortable with our new limitations. I don't see myself as sixty going on forty. I'm more like sixty going on sixty-five. I'm waiting for my friends to catch up so we will again have something in common. I see it, at least when I'm listening to old Lovin' Spoonful records, like the return of the golden age of the 1960s, when a whole generation felt communal, not competitive. Skinny-dipping is no longer an attractive option, but maybe we can all gather down at the joint-replacement clinic to feel that common bond. Younger people could yearn to get older faster to experience the fun we're having and not the other way around. It could be cool.

Given the emerging geriatric marketplace, there will probably be hundreds of lifestyles to choose from, from *Big Chill*-type communes with guardrails in every "pad" to do-it-yourself colon exams. And there will be lots of wheelchairs. Seas of wheelchairs. It'll be a wheelchair world. Manual chairs, power chairs, zippy three-wheel scooters with mud flaps, you name it. Like those "all-abilities" recreational parks every community in America has now built for disabled kids, there will be all-abilities housing developments, all-abilities vacation junkets, and all-abilities sports clubs and golf courses for adults. The world will catch up with Las Vegas, a place where they've known for years that there is money in wheelchairs and have catered to the every need of a rolling clientele. "More painkillers? A free tire check? No problem." A whole floor of IKEA will be devoted to adaptive living; people will be carting home roll-in showers in a box.

There's a print ad that runs every year in the *New Yorker* for one of the sleek department stores on Fifth Avenue. The store is gaily lighted, the snow is lightly falling, and a horde of shoppers are walking to and fro, moving fast and bundled tight. The first time I looked at that ad, I saw a different scenario: same store, same Hallmark backdrop, but every one of those excited consumers was in a wheelchair! Hundreds of wheelchair users rushing by, waving, smiling, full of holiday joy. OK, maybe as a polite nod to the rest of the world there are one or two walkers, but only a couple. In fact, off in a corner of the shot, a wheelchair user is giving a walker street directions to the all-abilities skating rink at Rockefeller Center. You can't discriminate, you know.

I'm starting to buy this vision of a wheelchair-centric universe and I hope you are too. Wheelchair culture—from adaptive SUVs to adaptive dude ranches to adaptive inverted-boomerang roller coasters—is only in its infancy. It will bloom into 1,000 new ways for wheelchair users to experience life. What this means for people like me is a more permanent sense of normality. We will have less and less reason to prove we are "just like regular people" by doing patently abnormal things like overworking or overplaying our physical limits. We will feel less defined by our disability because we will be less defined. The world will have adapted to us, not the other way around.

*　　*　　*

Perhaps the reason I feel so bullish about the future of wheel-chairs is that my own chances of walking again are nil or next to nil. That's part of the downside of becoming paralyzed after the age of fifty. Medical science is advancing at a furious clip to affect or conquer major diseases and disorders like spinal cord injury, Parkinson's, MS, juvenile-onset diabetes, and other evils, but it's not moving fast enough to ever get me back on my feet. And a lot of that has to do with the politics of stem cell research.

To most people who hear about or debate the stem cell controversy, it's a matter of values or religion. To people with disabilities, it's personal. And spirit-raising. When my doctor told me at the onset of my paralysis that I might walk again, this simple remark gave me enough of a charge to get me through the first year of my condition. The vaunted promise of stem cell regeneration, however distant the prospect, gives hope and courage to millions of people who are suffering or watching their loved ones suffer from the degenerative effects of a host of CNS afflictions. To many of these potential beneficiaries, arguing about the "ethics" of stem cell research while people are dying is like arguing about the Iraq war while your army buddy is bleeding to death. It's not the main issue.

The idea that the implantation of new cells into my back could enable me to walk again is not connected in my mind with any other larger social or political issue. It has nothing to do with left or right, Red or Blue, Christian or agnostic. It's cutting-edge medicine, like in vitro fertilization or heart transplants. And in the long run, all the current hand-wringing about "Brave New World" dystopias where stem cells are harvested and sold like Idaho potatoes will only delay the science, not eradicate it. Whether in California or Korea, the potential of stem cell research will be played out sooner or later, and if the promised breakthroughs actually occur, everyone will benefit. When and if stem cell procedures are accepted medical practice, it will take someone with enormous ideological conviction to say, "No, thanks, I think the use of embryonic stem cells is morally wrong, so please don't use this therapy on my twelve-year-old daughter with type 1 diabetes."

I guess my point is, put yourself in my shoes, so to speak, or try to see things from the perspective of those, like Nancy Reagan, who've had to witness the cruel consequences of Alzheimer's or some like disease and simply wish to spare others this agony. Stem cell "cures" may be a pipe dream, or it may be decades before we know if they live up to the hype. But to a fifteen-year-old who has just broken his back in a motorcycle accident, even help in 2020 could mean a much less diminished life. Again, to him, it's not about politics. It's about hope.

When you see stem cell research in this way, the future looks much brighter for some form of stem cell progress in America. As more aging citizens have firsthand experience of contracting Parkinson's, heart disease, or Alzheimer's, new forms of medical research will become more acceptable. It will probably be older people, facing physical frailty and disease, who will tip the balance in favor of the most aggressive research and younger people who will ultimately benefit.

Meanwhile, of course, few people of any age—and very few past age fifty—are waiting around for stem cells to save their lives. If age and frailty have a humanizing, even humbling, effect, as my experience suggests they do, then there is likely to be some immediate benefit, cure or no cure. A dear friend living in Menlo Park, California, Carol Doyle, spent the last years of her life battling a fierce form of cancer, inflammatory breast cancer. Her health, needless to say, was severely compromised. She spent most of every day in bed. Carol's advice to all her peers who dropped by to see her: do it now. Whatever it is you desire to do or be, or wherever you want to go, now's the time. In Carol's case, the urge was to keep working as an artist and merely adapt her art to her condition. Her artistic output after she contracted cancer was nothing short of spectacular; she cranked out pieces as if she was in a creative paroxysm. Or perhaps she was just focused. There's another sunny-side effect of illness—it helps you focus on what really brings you satisfaction. Insignificant things are now truly insignificant.

"Do it now." This sounds a lot like the Ram Dass mantra from the 1960s, "Be here now." Except it's a little more down-to-earth. The limits of illness and age invite distress and adapting to distress, but they also invite a freedom you probably always had but never exercised. The freedom to do what you want to do, even if it's wheelchair ballet.

Now is the best time in human history to be disabled. Compared with even a generation ago, let alone the dark ages of the nineteenth century, when a disability was often a ticket to a short, brutish life, we are living in handicapped heaven. At least in North America, there is less fear, prejudice, nervousness, and narrow-mindedness toward the disabled than ever before. You're still a minority, but then again, who isn't? As my son Max once said, if you're not "a white, walking male," you're a special-interest group. Healthy people have much more exposure now than in the past to the disabled, from Christopher Reeve and Michael J. Fox to Robert David Hall, the double amputee who picks over dead bodies as Dr. Al Robbins on *CSI*. There's now a kid in a wheelchair in almost every kids' movie that comes out, and studs in chairs show up even in Viagra commercials. The journalist John Hockenberry goes on the Jon Stewart show and the subject of his chair never comes up. It's been the law for over fifteen years to treat the disabled with dignity and respect, and except for some pockets of resistance, it's pretty much gone from "Do I have to?" to "Sure, we're all over it."

There are signs of this acceptance everywhere. The CBS TV affiliate in Chicago, WBBM, now has a regular designated "disability reporter" covering the disability beat. His name is Jim Mullen, and the segment is called the "Jim Mullen Report." Mullen is a quadriplegic former cop who was shot in the head and neck while on duty. He is paralyzed from the neck down and breathes with the assistance of a ventilator. According to the *Chicago Sun-Times*, he's the first quadriplegic to report regularly for any local television news operation in the country. My guess is that he will not be the last.

Of course, you could probably argue that all this is do-gooder window dressing, but I don't think so. I think "disability integration" is here to stay. Having said that, in no way do I want to minimize the enormous problems that disabled people, many of them poor and disenfranchised, go through daily—a criminal shortage of accessible housing and useful employment; too little health care, including help for alcohol and drug abuse; the vast prejudice that still exists against those with intellectual disabilities; and a lack of resources as simple as automotive hand controls so that people can drive to a clinic or to a job. Like the rest of the poor, a huge part of the disabled population is invisible, homebound, and without a safety net. If you can't drive to the unemployment office or catch a ride on accessible public transportation, you won't even make the jobless list.

But in terms of outright prejudice, inclusion is now at least an established social convention. Except among a few neo-Nazis in upper Idaho, the terms "disabled" and "inferior" are rarely mentioned in tandem. Subtle discrimination abounds, and is probably here to stay, but it's often indistinguishable from the broad muddy current of subtle discrimination directed against anyone who is different, therefore, scary, therefore, marginalized and ostracized. More often than not, a disabled person is in much the same boat as the gay or lesbian cousin the rest of the family walks on eggshells around, the geeky guy with the pink hair and the ring in his nose packing your groceries at Git & Go, the Jewish boyfriend who doesn't know the words to "Hark the Herald Angels Sing," or the Sikh merchant in a turban at the Better Business Bureau lunch. You're killed more often with kindness or neglect than meanness. People may still harbor ugly thoughts about you, but they will rarely express them out loud. It's just not done anymore. They may not give you a job or want you around, but they won't announce that you frighten, depress, or repulse them.

In the end, my own story, at least thus far, turned out to be a lot richer and more layered than a paralytic's version of *Black Like Me*. I had no choice in the matter, but if I had gone back to walking again, I would have certainly been more alert to the reality of the disabled but probably not a lot smarter about my own life. My empathy for the quad in the chair would have gone up, but I wouldn't know what's really going on inside his head. That's where I have a leg up, so to speak, on John Howard Griffin, the man who changed his skin color in *Black Like Me*. I got the whole experience, inside and out. I had to learn to live like this.

Looking back, here are a few general assumptions I think would apply to most people who find themselves in similar straits. First, your capacity to deal with any kind of severe ailment is probably much, much greater than you think. You have more emotional grit, more resolve, and greater perseverance than you imagine. Let me be the first to tell you: you are not the weak sister you think you are.

I don't know where so many people get the idea that they don't have what it takes to bear up under such stress. Maybe, as pass-the-chip-dip Americans, many of us have had so little true stress in our lives that it looms as more unbearable than it often is. The catastrophizing, in other words, is worse than the catastrophe. Or maybe it's just human nature to fear the unknown. Or maybe I'm just one of the fortunate "victims" of paralysis: one who had fifty-plus years to get ready; a career, however checkered; a family; and a relatively benign ailment. Also, like a light-skinned African-American, I could pass for "normal"—if you saw me only from the belly button up. I'm not bedridden for life. I've never had to drag my chair to a freeway off-ramp in search of a meal. I've never seen my legs blown off by a suicide bomber or had my seventeen-year-old back broken by a drunk driver or drive-by shooter. I wonder if I'd be so upbeat in the face of that.

Second, you have no idea how you'll deal with it until you deal with it. I guess you could prepare yourself by memorizing the Bible or Rabbi Kushner's *When Bad Things Happen to Good People*, but you'll forget and then you'll get blindsided and you'll be in the same situation as everyone else: "Jeez, this is weird—what do I do now?" The beauty of it is that this is a creative problem, not a follow-the-rulebook problem. You're not changing the oil; you're reinventing your life. You're a little messed up, sure, but you're also given a license to redefine yourself. You will concoct the solution, whatever it is, all on your own.

And it will most likely take a while. A long while. As much as you want to drop the subject and get on with it, you can't. My own experience is that the process unfolds pretty much without your conscious guidance. You can certainly inhibit it but probably not speed it up. For whatever reason, it takes the time it takes.

I'm only a few years into my so-called new incarnation, to use Ram Dass's lofty term, and I'm sure to have a few more to come, but if the other 75,999,999 people in my age bracket (and you know who you are) experience some of the same emotional shifts that I have in the face of ill health, you may be pleasantly surprised. You may find sources of strength you never knew you had. You may be liberated from lifelong fears and inhibitions. You may discover or rediscover a clear focus or passion, and pursue it sooner rather than later.

Or, on the other hand, you may be blown away by such an ugly twist of fate; learn to hate life; never bathe again; wallow in bitterness about every dime you didn't make, every opportunity you screwed up, and every fetching beauty or beau you didn't bed down; be hassled and humiliated by your aging, broken body and all the attendant indignities; and decide to drink or drug yourself into oblivion.

In any case, write and let us know how things turn out. And, by the way, the weather down here is just fine.

ACKNOWLEDGMENTS

I WOULD NOT HAVE SURVIVED the last nine years, let alone written this book, without the love, support, help, and friendship of the following people: Drs. Norman Lavet, Daniel Rovner, James Daniel, Alan Engelberg, Gary Leach, Joel Aronowitz, Stephen Uman, Biao Lu, Ralph Potkin, and the indispensable Letty Hoffman; John Rigney, Charles Clancy, John Ferriter, Jared Levine, Tony Eaton, Dan Harris, Mark Oswald, Andrew Solt, Barbara Corday, David Chase, Ilene Landress, Carmi Zlotnik, Russell Schwartz, and a dozen others at HBO; Eleanor and Rowland Miller, great thanks, the Open Charter School community, Ted Steinberg and Ellen Brown, Martin and Wendy Mull, Harry Shearer, Bill and Robin King, John Lynn, Bill and Sherry Conger, Harold Ramis, Ann Ramis, Kit Sibert, Jodi Sibert, Megan Williams, Michael Shamberg, Kevin and Claudia Bright, Julia Liebeskind, Paula Charlton, Donna Miyahara, Judye Kaplan, Coke Sams, Dub Cornett, Eric and Carol Doyle, Robert and Marguerite Kenner, Paul and Pita

Goldsmith, Tom Green, Ben Stein, Jimmy Kimmel, and Tom Shales; superagent Jay Mandel, who launched this book and introduced me to the best editor I've ever had, Gail Winston; Charlotte Wasserstein, Anna Weissman, and the invaluable assistance of Maitreya Friedman (the one in the red dress on the cover); and most of all, my family, Ralph and Sherry Rucker, Louise and Jim Connor, too many nieces and nephews to name, and my dear Ann-Marie, Blaine, and Max.